Prayer is a Way of Life

Prayer is a Way of Life

edited by
Marion Stroud

Pickering Paperbacks

Contents

Foreword

In 1911 a young Russian woman, Barbara, was very worried about her father's safety, during a period of political instability in Russia. She asked a monk of the Russian Orthodox Church to pray for her father and while he was doing so the monk had a vision. Among other things he told Barbara that he had seen Russia in the grip of a godless ideology; that in the last days Germany would be divided in two and that America would feed the world. He also said that Britain would lose her Empire and her colonies and would come to almost total ruin, but would be saved by praying women.

When I read about this in Lance Lambert's book *Battle for Israel*, I had the uneasy feeling that if God was depending on my prayers to save Britain, the outlook for the country was not very hopeful! In common with many others, I am painfully aware that although I know what I should do, the ideal and the reality are still so widely separated.

This is why I found editing this book both a challenge and a comfort. Many of the contributors have progressed far further along the way of prayer than I have, and I have been excited by what God has done in their lives and challenged to let his Spirit have greater freedom to work in and through me. But I have also been comforted to know that there are those who have been greatly used by God, who still ask the same questions and grapple with the same problems of time-pressure, distractions, doubt and dryness, as I experience in prayer.

And so I am encouraged to try again, and to pray with a renewed vision of what God can do. For this is perhaps where we fail most often: we pray, but we don't honestly think that it will make much difference. So my prayer for myself and for all those who contributed to, or will read this book, is for *expectant* faith. Faith that will enable us to ask and expect God to do a new thing in our lives, releasing us from the fear that going on with him may lead us into situations that we can't handle. God is able to do far more than we can calculate – both in us, and in those to whom he sends us . . . Dare we ask him to? Will we pray for victory in areas in which we have previously known defeat, confident that it will come; expect to be led to people who are already prepared and waiting for what we have to share with them, and expect to find new opportunities for love and service in the most unlikely situations?

God is raising up an army of praying women, but new recruits are desperately needed. There is no age-limit, and the only qualifications for active service are willing hearts and a vision. A vision of the needs of a sin-sick society and a vision of what God can and will do in response to our prayers. I think it was Winston Churchill in World War *II* who said '*Give us the tools, and we will finish the job.*' Prayer is the mightiest tool of all – what a challenge to realise that God wants ordinary women to wield it, in order to help bring in his Kingdom.

MARION STROUD

Prayer is a matchless opportunity
 Through prayer
  People
   Things
    Problems and Relationships can be transformed.
Prayer has infinite power – because it is directed to an infinitely powerful God.

Mother Basilea Schlink.

8

Contributors' Who's Who

Marion Ashton and her husband Leigh are both medical doctors. They spent a number of years in Kenya, first as missionaries with the *Africa Inland Mission* and secondly, while still in close fellowship with the mission, in a private practice where they were able to work among both Africans and the expatriate community. They returned to England in 1964 and, with the family grown up, Marion has been increasingly involved in counselling people, mainly Christians, with all kinds of problems. She also speaks on such subjects as pastoral couselling, coping with stress etc., to church groups and teaches those preparing for Christian work.

Sue Barnett was born and grew up in South London. Trained in Physical Education she has taught in schools in Wandsworth, Enfield and Ilford. She serves as chairman of Bournemouth and Christchurch Christian Lunch and Dinner Club. Although heavily involved in conference and seminar ministry, she remains committed to sharing her faith with her friends and neighbours. Along with her husband Doug and teenage sons, Stephen and Duncan, she lives in Christchurch, Dorset. After using Keepfit groups as an opportunity to build deep relationships and introduce Jesus naturally to her friends, she is currently working on a record and tape entitled, *Fit for Life*.

Fiona Castle was born in West Kirby, Wirral, where her father was a GP. The youngest in a family of four, she trained from the age of nine at Elmhurst Ballet School, a boarding school in Camberley, Surrey. After leaving school she danced in several pantomimes and summer seasons, eventually graduating from chorus to 'principal girl'. She was in the original cast of the *Sound of Music* when she met Roy. They married in 1963 and now have four children, Daniel (18), Julia (17), Antonia (14) and Benjamin

9

(10). She enjoys dressmaking, needlework and gentle forms of 'middle-aged' exercise such as jogging, swimming, squash and keep-fit!

Margaret Cundiff is a Deaconess in the Church of England and lives in Selby, Yorkshire. Her husband Peter is a businessman and they have two teenage children, Julian and Alison. She is Broadcasting Officer for the Diocese of York and broadcasts regularly on a number of radio stations. She is a member of the General Synod of the Church of England as well as of committees on communications. She has written three books, *Called to be me*, *Following on* and, the latest, *I'd like you to meet* . . . (to be published by Triangle Books, autumn 1984).

Margaret Dehqani-Tafti was born to missionary parents in Iran, where she lived throughout her childhood. After doing some nursing in England, she returned to Iran and married there. Her husband was the first Persian bishop of the Episcopal church in Iran, and they lived there with their four children until the Islamic Revolution which began in 1978. In 1979 an assassination attempt was made on the Bishop, and their only son was murdered. The Dehqani-Taftis now live in Basingstoke, where Margaret is helping her husband as he combines three jobs as Bishop of Iran (in exile), President Bishop of the Episcopal Church in the Middle East, and the Assistant Bishop in Winchester.

Born in 1942 in Kent, **Meryl Doney** has had a wide variety of job experience, including advertising, working for the Christian news magazine *Crusade* (now called *Today*), the Mayflower Family Centre in East London, Bible college, student welfare work, Travelling Secretary for Universities and Colleges Christian Fellowship with special responsibility for art, music and drama students, and as an editor for Lion Publishing. Married to journalist Malcolm Doney, she has two children and lives in North London. She has written some 32 books for children and now works as a freelance writer, family commitments permitting.

Pat King is an American author living in Kent, Washington. She is the wife of her childhood sweetheart, Bill, the mother of ten children, and the author of eight books and three Bible studies. She is best known to both American and British readers for her

10

book on time management for homemakers, *How Do You Find the Time?* (Pickering & Inglis). Mrs. King was educated at Seattle University and studied writing under the tutelege of Barbara Large, well known Hampshire writing teacher. She and her family attend St. Philomena's Catholic Church in Des Moines, Washington. She is currently working on a Christian romantic novel.

Gail Lawther is presently editor of *Christian Woman* magazine. She spent her childhood in many different locations, which has given her a liking for new horizons and a varied life, and trained for a career at Reading University. She spent three years as a book editor/author for a secular publishing company before branching out into embroidery and magazine work. Her husband Christopher is a typographic designer.

Faith Lees is one of the founder members of *Post Green Community*. She and her husband Sir Tom Lees have lived at Post Green for many years, and have seen it change from a family home open to those looking for God, into the centre of an ecumenical, life-style community, where those who come find stimulation and healing. Prayer and counselling have been her main work in the past 15 years. Faith was a JP, and has written two books, *Love is our Home*, with Jeanne Hinton and *Break Open my World*, with Val. Nobbs. She has 4 children and 4 grandchildren.

Jean Raddon is an English woman, although currently living in Australia. She did her nursing training in London after which she spent four years in the Queen Alexandra's Imperial Military Service, serving on the Continent and in India.
Once demobilised she developed an increasing, compelling interest in missionary work, trained at Redcliffe Missionary Training College and was part of the first medical team to enter Nepal. She worked there for seventeen years with the *International Nepal Fellowship*.
Jean is now working in Australia with *Christian Women's Conventions International* as Overseas Promotion Officer. Having written a book on her experiences in Nepal, she is currently engaged in writing Bible studies, speaking at conventions, counselling women, recording cassettes of various kinds and speaking on radio programmes. With her friend Mary, Jean also finds time to travel

and visit isolated groups of women, bringing Christian literature and leading Bible Studies.

Jan Ramsey is married with two grown-up children. With her help her husband Vic founded a successful work amongst drug addicts in 1964 called *New Life Foundation Trust*.

Converted to Christ in her late teens, Jan was very actively involved in the world of the theatre and singing.

An experienced broadcaster and counsellor, Jan is National President of the *British Women's Aglow Fellowship* and also is a member of the *International Board of Women's Aglow Fellowship International* which has its headquarters in Seattle, Washington, USA. Jan was invited to pioneer this exciting ministry and outreach to women in 1980 in the British Isles and there are now close to 30 Chapters scattered throughout the country.

Sue Sinclair was born in a remote corner of Kenya, where her parents were missionaries. She has always loved outdoor life and open spaces. After graduating from Keele University, she married Max Sinclair, director of Hildenborough Hall Christian Conference Centre.

Sue's faith in God was challenged and deepened through her husband's sudden paralysis as the result of a car crash. This meant adjustments in attitudes and life style. She enjoys being a housewife and mother of Naomi (13), Anna (12) and Ben (8); she runs a weekly Crusader Club for children in her home, keeps a variety of animals, and grows lots of vegetables.

Patricia St John was born in England in 1919. Her father was a Bible teacher and she was one of five children. Her childhood was a very happy one.

On leaving school, she worked for four years as a teacher-trainee in a junior school, and then trained as a nurse at St Thomas's Hospital, London. In 1949 she went out to Morocco and worked as a missionary nurse till 1976. She had a special interest in needy children and babies suffering from malnutrition.

In 1976 Patricia returned home to look after an elderly, invalid relative. That is what she is doing now but she hopes one day to return to Morocco. She has written a number of books and is a much-loved children's author.

Anne Townsend is a doctor and the mother of three children aged 18, 20, and 22. Her husband John is a surgeon and works full-time for *Tear Fund* as their Medical and Health Care Consultant. Both worked overseas for the Overseas Missionary Fellowship as medical missionaries in Thailand for sixteen years. Ann is currently editor of *Family* Magazine.

Caroline Urquhart is married with three teenage children. Her husband Colin is a well-known preacher and author of several books. Together they have been involved in spiritual renewal and revival for many years. Caroline's first book, *His God, My God*, was an immediate best-seller. It tells of her spiritual pilgrimage with her husband and children from a parish-based ministry to establishing an ecumenical community in Sussex, concerned to bring new life, faith and healing in Jesus to the nations.

Eileen Vincent is married has one married daughter and two sons, the youngest now 12 years old. She lives in Hertfordshire where she is closely involved with her husband Alan's church planting ministry.
Eileen is the author of two books, *God Can Do It here, and Something's Happening*, besides having a speaking ministry which is widely appreciated. For 6 years she edited *Outpouring* magazine, published in Bombay. Eileen and her husband have a special love for India where they served as missionaries for 10 years. Eileen has a continuing contact through regular visits.

Christine Wood is the author of thirteen children's books. She has also written her autobiography and numerous devotional and inspirational articles for both British and American periodicals. For the past eleven years she has been British Associate Editor of *Decision Magazine*. Christine is married to the historical biographer Douglas Wood.

1 Fiona Castle:
How Prayer Became my Way of Life

'Don't worry about anything; instead pray about everything; tell
God your needs and don't forget to thank him for the answers.
If you do this you will experience God's peace, which is far more
wonderful than the human mind can understand. His peace will
keep your hearts and minds quiet and at rest as you trust in Christ
Jesus'.

(Philippians 4. 6–7 TLB)

I have always prayed! I remember my mother praying with me
at night when I was very small, teaching me poems, such as,
'*Gentle Jesus, Meek and Mild*' and '*Jesus, Tender Shepherd Hear
Me* . . .' I was very proud to have learnt to say them off by heart!

When I went to boarding school, I prayed . . . The 'religious'
side of school life was very important, so we were encouraged to
attend chapel regularly and woe betide anyone who missed
morning assembly! We even had a 'Prayer bell', morning and
evening, when we had to drop to our knees instantly, wherever
we were and pray briefly! Afterwards we would vie with each
other for the funniest story about what we had been doing at the
time the bell went.

When I entered the world of Show Business, I prayed . . .
mainly selfish prayers; that I would get the audition or part I was
trying for, or that the show I was in would run so that I wouldn't
have to join the dole queue! I prayed that God would find me a
husband, because I dreaded the thought of becoming an 'Old
Maid'!

When I met Roy and we married, I was embarrassed to admit
to him that I prayed, in case he mocked me, but he accepted it
and willingly came with me to church, whenever possible.

When our children were born, I began the pattern all over
again with them, praying by their bedsides at night, using glossily
illustrated prayerbooks, with many well-worn favourites. We took

them to church too, wanting to share with them the faith we had then. At that time Roy had the reality without the ritual and, I realise now, that I had the ritual without the reality.

Reading through this might lead you to believe that I was a fairly pious sort of person, but I confess to you that my prayer life had never matured beyond the childhood style of praying. It would either be prayers from a prayer book or the 'God bless Mummy and Daddy' sort of extemporary prayer!

Then a wonderful thing happenned. My world and my life started to fall apart. Although this was not wonderful while it was happening, for the first time in my life God was able to become real to me.

I was suffering from severe depression, which caused me to become very withdrawn. I had had bouts of depression from my teenage years, but with each successive child that I had, it became worse, so that some days life became unbearable. I must have become pretty painful to live with too, and, looking back I am amazed that Roy put up with me the way he did.

He gave me everything I needed to make life pleasant and happy. I had a lovely home with all the labour-saving devices that could be provided. I had four beautiful, healthy children, so I really had nothing to be depressed about. I was aware of this, and the knowledge of it only served to make me worse, because of the guilt I felt at being so depressed. It was a vicious circle of tiredness, depression and guilt, wrapped up in a big helping of self-pity.

Roy was away from home a good deal at this stage, so I was left to cope on my own with four small children. This I was able to do quite adequately, although since I lived on nervous energy, I collapsed in a big heap once Roy returned, not providing the loving atmosphere he would have expected!

At the same time as maintaining the home in Roy's absence, I felt it was my duty to become involved with various activities connected with the church and the community. So although I found it difficult to mix socially, I would force myself to take on all sorts of commitments outside the home, thus depriving the children of my undivided attention.

I believed at the time, and so wrongly, that I had to 'earn' my way to heaven by the way I worked for others. I didn't consider the fact that my family was suffering as a result. As I look back, I realise that I was so busy pushing them into a slot to suit my convenience that I didn't spend time getting to know their needs, their fears, their hopes and their problems. I was too wrapped up in my own problems to notice.

The same was true where Roy was concerned. I didn't take time to share his needs and frustrations and the problems with his work. He went his way and I went mine, not concerned with the situations he had to face. With his particular lifestyle, being exposed to the media wherever he went, he needed to have the comfort and security of a loving atmosphere to return to.

So I tried praying – but it was more as an act of discipline than the possibility that I had a loving heavenly Father who delighted in the prayers of his children. I used to pray for the things I wanted and for things to happen in the way I wanted them to happen. I suppose it was not much different from making a wish and hoping it would come true. Even going to church was a form of discipline and not from a desire to worship God. My mother had always taught me to 'set a good example', and I supposed this was one way of carrying that out. Roy was right, when, on occasions he would say, 'I don't know why you bother to go to church. By the time you've got all the children ready you're in such a bad temper, it can't possibly do you any good.' But I would get to the church and smile at everyone, making out that everything was wonderful!

I believed in God and I believed in Jesus, although I looked on the Gospel story as more of a historical document than a living reality. I didn't think there was anything in it that could help me with my problems on a Monday morning. It was all too vague and distant, with a set of rules which were far too difficult to be kept. I would say all the prayers on a Sunday, then carry on doing my own thing for the rest of the week.

However, I reached the stage where the rest of the week was unbearable. I was tense, nervous, depressed, unable to make the smallest decision without panic. I had had enough of life as it was. I was beginning to admit to myself that my life was a mess, but I didn't know where to turn. If this was all there was to life, what was the point? Somewhere, somehow there had to be something more.

It was at this point that I turned to God for help and I prayed the most meaningful prayer I had ever prayed. This time it was a desperate cry for help and it was from the heart, not just the head.

17

I remember that it was on 25 February, 1975, when I returned from taking the children to school. Only the youngest, Benjamin, who was sixteen months old, was still at home. I went upstairs to my bedroom and shut the door. I got down on my knees and I cried out to God, saying 'God, if you're there at all, you've *got* to help me and you've got to help me *now*, because I've had it; I can't cope any more.' That's all – just a cry from the heart which I didn't expect God to hear, let alone answer. But he did – and within a minute, because no sooner had I stood up than the phone rang. The person speaking said that she wasn't sure why she was phoning me but she thought perhaps we ought to get together. She invited me to coffee sometime so that we could have a chat . . . She was someone I hardly knew, in fact we had only met once, but I did know she was a committed Christian. I agreed to meet her the following week and I put the phone down. Then I stopped and I realised that moments before, I had been on my knees, crying to God for help and immediately help was being offered. There couldn't have been a clearer answer to prayer than that!

I rang back immediately and asked her if I could go and see her straight away. She agreed, so, having thrust the baby in Roy's arms and told him I was going out, I found my way to her house. I then poured out all my problems to this loving, gentle Christian. My problems which were so ordinary and unspectacular . . . loneliness – emptiness – confusion – depression – tiredness – these were the problems I shared with her. It was probably the first time I had been able to be honest with anyone. I had always been so ashamed of the emotions I felt – thinking that no one else ever had problems of this nature, especially one who was fortunate enough to have a kind loving husband and a good home (how common my problems were, I have been discovering ever since!).

When I had finished, she asked me the most important question of my life:

'Even though you are a church-goer, have you actually ever stopped and asked Jesus to take over your life?'

'No' I replied, non-plussed.

'Well, don't you think it's about time you did?'

'Yes,' I replied, bewildered and rather embarrassed, wondering where all this would lead.

She then read Revelation 3.20 from her Bible.

'*Look! I have been standing at the door and I am constantly knocking. If anyone hears me calling him and opens the door, I will come in and enjoy fellowship with him and he with Me'*

She suggested that Jesus had been knocking at the door of my heart for thirty-five years and I had never actually asked him in. I had paid lip-service to him in the reciting of prayers, psalms and hymns but I didn't have a living vital relationship with the one who had died for me on the cross.

So, there and then I asked Jesus to take over my life. I became aware of the hopeless mess I had made of everything that was most precious to me, and asked him to forgive me. Even as I was praying I could not be sure that this decision would make things any different. I remember thinking that I would have to try terribly hard to be better, to raise my standards and give up things in order to try to lead a better life! However, I was also aware that I had tried everything else and nothing had worked, my back was against the wall, so anything was worth a try.

I need not have worried, for the moment I took that step, I became aware of the most beautiful peace, flooding every part of me, so that the tensions which had built up in me over the months just seemed to melt away. I seemed to be melting too, letting go of all my burdens and allowing Jesus to carry them for me.

I know that at that moment I was different. In 2 Corinthians 5.17 it says,

'When someone becomes a Christian he becomes a brand new person inside. He is not the same anymore. A new life has begun'.
And that was true of me.

Although I had read the story of Nicodemus in the Bible and Jesus's command to him to be born again, I had never realised that it was relevant to my own life. Either I was too blind, or had never been shown, or had thought it was all part of the Anglican Baptism and Confirmation; I'm not sure and I don't think it matters. What does matter is that we realise the significance and importance of this spiritual re-birth and don't just drift through life, as I had done, with a vague concept of how to believe in God.

God answered my prayers on that day and now I know I can trust him with every detail of my life. It's rather like handing over the steering wheel of the car, and sitting in the passenger seat. I know that I can relax and allow Jesus to drive me safely to my destination, because he loves me and knows the best route for my life. I spent so long at the steering wheel, so tense and fearful, wondering which way to turn, thinking I could control my own life. If only I had realised sooner what a waste of time and energy it was, living that way, life could have been so different.

So, what has happened to my prayer life now? I have to admit that I don't have all the answers. I am human and as such am subject to mistakes and failures. But the Bible does have all the answers, and so it is now my 'Handbook' to life. I know that when in doubt or trouble I can go running to that handbook and God will supply the answer I need through it. It is not always the answer that I would like to have, but it is the one which will set me back on the road that leads to 'life'.

I know that God is always there, ready to answer me and to forgive me when I ask. He cares about everything, however seemingly small and insignificant. The Bible tells us that the Holy Spirit will lead us into all truth (John 16.13). This I have certainly found to be the case. The Holy Spirit shows me where I am going wrong, and through prayer, how to go about changing. This was one of the most surprising things to me when I first became a Christian, because, far from having to try harder to be good, I found that the Holy Spirit was leading me to change things; helping me to see things from a different perspective; showing me that things which before had seemed very important to me became less important, and other, seemingly less important things became priorities.

'Seek ye first the Kingdom of God . . .'.

Whereas before I had read the Bible and prayed as an act of discipline, I now found that a quiet time of reading and prayer was a 'must'. I was discovering new truths and realities and meaning for my life to-day from every page. I longed to be with other Christians, with whom there would be an immediate rapport and bond, even if we had not met before. This I have found in all the countries I have visited since; not just in the local community.

I find that if I seek God first, it saves so much time, worry and uncertainty. I don't think that the verse about 'Seeking God's Kingdom First' just means praying at the beginning of the day, although I, personally, have found that to be very necessary; but in every situation, if we seek God's guidance and desire for us before we take the matter into our own hands, churning it over and weighing up the pros and cons he will show us how to make the right decision.

Sometimes if I am busy, I start rushing through my prayers, making my requests like a shopping list! I read somewhere that if we are too busy to pray, we are far busier than God intended us to be! I then have to stop and take time to listen to God and be quiet so that he can speak to me. I have found that effective praying must be a two way conversation. We soon get tired of someone who does all the talking in a conversation, don't we? I believe God must feel like that when we rattle off our needs to him without allowing him the time to tell us what he wants of us. This involves stopping and asking him to speak to us, then allowing him the time to do so. Many times God has spoken to me in prayer as I have brought some particular need or problem to him and then just focused all my attention on him, waiting . . . in *silence*. Sometimes the answer is 'wait'. At other times it is a feeling or impression of what I should do. And at others, words come into my mind that are as clear as if God is dictating to me so that I have been able to write them down and refer to them at later times.

When my children were smaller, I remember once complaining to one of the Pastors of our church, that if I didn't rise before anyone else in the household was awake, to pray and read the Bible, I could rarely find another place in the day which would be undisturbed, such was the chaos at the time with four young children! However, this dear man of God quoted the twenty-third Psalm to me.

'I will lead you beside still waters . . .' and explained that a shepherd always went ahead of his sheep to seek out a place for them to drink and rest, otherwise, when they became thirsty they would drink whatever was nearby, possibly stagnant and contaminated, thus making themselves ill.

'The Good Shepherd', he said, 'Is just like that. He will provide a place of still waters for you if you ask. But you must recognise it and take it immediately. Don't wait till you have finished a job or the moment will pass.'

How true that has been! Many times I have had the vacuum cleaner in my hands and have heard God saying, 'Now!' and have dropped everything to pray. If I ignore the call, I find that work crowds in and the still moment has been squeezed out.

I also have to be careful not to crowd God out of a day because of a schedule I have set for myself. Sometimes I ask God to help himself to my day, then I go on to tell him all the things I think are important!

If I really allow the Holy Spirit to guide me, he sometimes turns my day upside down, showing me very firmly that my ways are not his ways. Such joy comes with obedience on those occasions.

I remember once, to my shame, that I was in a very rebellious frame of mind. Nothing seemed to be going right and my prayers seemed to be bouncing back off the ceiling! So I dared to say to God that I wouldn't pray to him or refer to him for the rest of the day unless he proved to me that I couldn't get along without him. Well God certainly did prove his existence and my need of him, because I couldn't count the number of times I found myself automatically and subconsciously turning to him to pray. I have never doubted since and although I don't recommend it to anyone as a way of proving the existence of God, he was gracious enough to allow my little exercise and to answer my prayer very emphatically, to prove my need of him.

There was a time, in August 1980, when the power and effectiveness of faithful and persistent prayer became very evident to me and to my family as a whole. Our son Daniel, then aged fifteen, fell from a cliff onto a rock beneath, on his head. It was in the Isle of Man, where Roy was working at the time. He was taken to hospital and put in the Intensive Care Unit, where he was on the critical list for several days. I immediately 'phoned our Pastor at home, asking him to start praying for Daniel. This started a chain of prayer, which spread throughout the church fellowship.

The following day, Justin Dennison, one of the pastors and Malcolm Richard, an elder from our church, flew over to be with us, and they prayed with Daniel and annointed him with oil as the Bible tells us we can do when people are sick. (James 5.14). Having been unconscious, with only fleeting moments of awareness, he responded to their prayers by looking up and saying 'Amen!' This began the slow but steady healing process, so that, within two weeks he was able to climb the steps of the pulpit, with the aid of a walking stick, to praise God for his healing and to thank the fellowship for their prayers. The love and concern of so many people, together with the dedicated attention of a wonderful, skillful medical staff, seemed to me to be God's way of showing us how much he cared for us all, as we trusted him for every detail of that traumatic episode.

Although Roy has never sought publicity, this was one time

when his links with the media gave the opportunity for thousands, yes, thousands, to join us in prayer for Daniel's healing. We are still hearing to-day, of individuals, prayer groups and church fellowships who were moved to pray for Daniel at that time. In the first week alone, I acknowledged over three hundred letters from people showing their concern. We know God allowed that accident to happen for many reasons. We just had to trust him at the time to work his purposes out through it. We have heard since of people who have come into a personal relationship with Jesus as a result; of healed family relationships, when people realise how fragile life is, and that 'Now' is the only moment we can be sure of.

God also showed us areas in our lives where we had our priorities wrong, teaching us to totally put our trust in him because 'He holds the future.' He showed us that every person is very precious to him, whatever their social and education level. Daniel was and is very special to him and we must pray, not that our children will be the brightest and best, but that they will be able to find out what God wants them to do. We don't need to fight and struggle to achieve what to the world would seem acceptable. So much of what we want for our children, I have discovered, is for our own pride and satisfaction.

God prepared me for Daniel's fall by showing me earlier in that same day, that our peace and joy are dependent on our relationship with him and not on our wordly circumstances. He gave me an opportunity to put it into practice very quickly! It was a beautiful and timely lesson, so that all through the crisis I was able to breathe in God's peace, where all around there was chaos and confusion!

However, it is easy to slip back into trying instead of trusting, so it is good to be able to reflect on times when God has held me firm in difficult circumstances. He is Almighty God, who can be trusted with every part of our lives; that is what he wants – every part of our lives.

I have a little book mark in my Bible which says, 'Seek the presence of Jesus. Through him will everything be solved which you yourself cannot solve' and that I have proved to be gloriously true.

2 Pat King:
But How do you Spend the Time in Prayer?

'How would you like to go for a long ride tomorrow?' My husband, Bill, was inviting me to go with him while he made a sales call. It was to be a two-hour ride, I'd sit in the car for about two hours and wait for him then we'd have dinner and drive home together.

I jumped at the chance, the most appealing part being the two-hour wait. I was in the middle of a writing project and a two-hour period without interruption seemed made to order.

The next day, a day as cold as January can be, Bill left me sitting in the car parked on a busy street. Beside me on the seat were a sheaf of papers and a thermos of tea. 'Don't hurry,' I told him. 'I have plenty to keep me busy.'

First I finished up the last few pages of the book I'd brought along, *What Happens When Women Pray* by Evelyn Christiansen. Then I closed my eyes and prayed as I always do before starting work, committing both my family and my work to the Lord. Opening my eyes I poured some tea and picked up my folder of manuscript papers. 'Good heavens, *no!*' I exclaimed. I'd brought the wrong folder! I'd left my writing project and research at home.

What was I to do? I felt so lost, so annoyed. It was too cold to go for a nice long walk; I couldn't write without my notes. Finally I settled on re-reading the book I'd brought along on the importance of prayer.

As I read, there in the quiet, without the interruptions, without the pressure of 'having to get busy' I heard the Lord's voice. What I heard in my heart couldn't have surprised me more. 'I want you to tithe your time in prayer on days when you are alone.'

For a moment time seemed to stand still. To this day I can still picture the trees etched on the cold horizon, the people passing in the crosswalk, the traffic halting for a stop light. 'Me, Lord? Tithe my time?'

The answer was yes.

At home the next day I figured out that a tithe (a tithe is 10%) of twenty-four hours was two hours and twenty-four minutes. It seemed utterly extravagant, like buying a Rolls Royce when taking the Underground had always worked out fine before. Yet I knew I had not imagined the voice I'd heard in the car.

The next day as soon as the family, Bill and our last five children, were off to school or work, I knelt beside my bed and began to pray. I'd prayed regularly but never lengthily so this was a totally new experience. I prayed every prayer I knew, for all my children and for every person I could think of that had asked for prayer. When I was through I opened up my eyes. Twenty minutes had gone by. I still had two hours and four minutes left to go.

I struggled through it. The next day and the next I did the same. It was much more an exercise in perservance than it was in prayer. Yet, in time, I learned how to fill two hours and twenty-four minutes so that it became a blessing in my life and an eventual blessing to my whole family.

Before going any further I want to clarify one important thing. At first I tried to pray this length of time every day but I soon learned that some days lengthy prayer is impossible. I was relieved to read over my notes and see the words, 'on days that you are alone.'

I know that I should never leave a child alone, a baby fussing, a husband to fend for himself while I pray. It really *can* be only on days when I am alone. But even on those days I soon found this kind of commitment could only be met if I did not postpone it. If I said, 'I'll do it after the washing up or when this job here is done, it only loses the prayer time in the details of the day. It's like the jelly mix that gets lost on the wrong shelf and isn't found until it's too late in the day for it to jell. I soon learnt that I must start early enough so I can get to my writing at a reasonable time.

I began to bring along to prayer a Bible, a notebook and a scratch pad. The notebook is to record anything I might hear the Lord speak or any thoughts I want to write to him. The scratch pad is for all the 'urgent' thoughts that distract: buy carrots, ring up Maryann, defrost meat. Once noted they are out of my mind and my prayer. I brought the Bible because I've found a Bible is an integral part of prayer.

Praise

Gradually I developed a flexible pattern with praise, thanksgiving, listening, intercession and my needs in succession. This formula I am about to share with you works just as well for ten minutes if that's all the time available.

It seemed fitting to begin with praise. Psalms 8, 66, 100, 145–150 are all good psalms of praise to start out on. I've chosen to pick one a day and to sing it aloud. Now the Lord has not blessed me with a golden voice, aluminum would describe it best. But I have not let that deter me from singing to the Lord in a melody composed, however off key, on the spot. I sing it once as written, a second time repeating my favourite phrases and a third time inserting my name. Here's an example:

> Hallelujah, Yes praise the Lord!
> Sing him a new song, Pat,
> Sing his praises, Pat.
> O, Pat, rejoice in your maker
>   O, Pat, exult in your king. (Psalm 149.1–3 adapted!)

As you can see, it's quite a lot of fun but more than that, praise clears the mind of the demands of the moment and focuses it on the Lord. When you have a long time set aside for prayer you can praise for a long period. If you have only the interlude while the baby naps you can adjust the moments you give to praise to that amount of time. However long there is for prayer, starting with praise puts God in his rightful position. Praise says that God is Lord of all and it declares his kingship in our lives.

Praise focuses us on God and our relationship to him. It says, You are the Creator; I am the created. You are the Shepherd; I am the sheep. You are the Father; I am the daughter.

'*The Lord is present wherever people praise him*' (Psalm 22.3). What better way to begin our prayer time than to open our Bibles and praise the name of the Lord?

Thanksgiving

A young woman once said to me, 'I don't need to take a special time for 'Thank you' prayers. All I have to do is look into the faces of my children or look out the window and see the handiwork of God and I am thankful.'

Day in and day out I wonder if this really works. What if the children have completely done you in with fretting or quarrels? What if God's handiwork has been ten straight days of grey drizzle? For me it works much better to have the time set aside for giving thanks.

To do this I've made a list, a rather long one that I can refer to, of people and blessings for which I am grateful. I'll share three items from this list here. One: I'm thankful for the groceries in our stores and markets. Not too long ago I read of a Russian cosmonaut who had defected from Russia. Part of his orientation in the free world was to visit a large grocery store.

Up to that point he had been suspicious that what he had been shown was an inflated and unreal view of life outside the Soviet Union. When he arrived at the grocery store and saw the displays of eggs, butter and cheese he said to himself. "Now I know they are lying to me, I know such abundance does not really exist". It took a number of trips to other stores before he really understood that what you and I take for granted was *real*.

'*Thank you, God, for groceries.*'

Two: I'm grateful for my teenage daughter, Katy, whose last few years have alternated between tears, power struggles, great hurts and sudden bursts of unaccountable happiness. She is either going up or going down and I am in the middle, buffeted, whichever way she goes. One day I prayed, '*O, God, do something with this girl. She is driving me crazy!*' (Honest prayers are most often not the beautiful ones!)

In time I understood that I was to be thankful for her. '*Dear Lord, thank you for this daughter. Thank you for her tears because she's growing through them. Thank you for what I'm learning in patience as her mother. Thank you for the times she is cheery. Thank you for your plan for her life*'.

One evening I sat beside her bed and prayed all these thank you's out loud. 'O, Mum', she said, 'you *do* understand, don't you?' And now that I think about it, I guess I do.

'*Thank you, God, for Katy.*'

Three: I'm grateful that God sent Jesus to die for me, but not just for me but for my son, Paul. Paul was not a perfect person and when he was killed in an accident I knew he had done very little to earn heaven. The best thing Paul had going for him was that he was a believer. Paul believed that Jesus had died for him and because of that belief I am at peace (see John 3.16).

'*Thank you, God, for sending Jesus.*'

When Jesus lived on earth he gave the example of his own thankfulness. At the tomb of Lazarus he gave thanks; '*Father, I thank you that you have heard me . . .*' (John 11.41). In feeding the multitude, '*. . . he took the seven loaves and gave thanks.*' (Mark 8.6). Paul the Apostle tells us, '*In everything give thanks . . .*' (1 Thessalonians 5.18).

Yes, let's be thankful in everything. And when thanksgiving is built into the day's schedule and there's a list before us, no day can go by without telling the Father that we are thankful.

Listening

So far I've done most of the talking. Now I need to be quiet. But before I begin to listen I pray this psalm:

'*Search me, O God, and know my heart;*
test my thoughts.
Point out anything you find in me
that makes you sad . . .' (Psalm 139.23, 24)

So often, in the following silence I've heard the Lord speak. '*Daughter, what you said on the phone yesterday was gossip.*' Or, '*Daughter, there's bitterness in your heart.*'

Once a sin is illuminated it can be dealt with. '*Father, I turn my back on the sin of gossip. I'm sorry. Will you forgive me?*' We are promised that if we confess our sins to him that he is faithful to forgive us and clean our lives (1 John 1.9).

When there is room in our prayer time for God to search us (remember we aren't psychologists, we don't search ourselves) and for us to respond, we go to prayer one kind of a person and get up from our knees another. We kneel down with sin in our lives and rise up with it gone (Isaiah 1.18).

When we are quiet before God he can speak to us about other matters. We do hear his voice. '*My sheep know my voice . . .*' Jesus promises (John 10.4). This is the time for pencil and notebook because writing down what the Lord speaks to us is a long lasting reminder that he does really care about our lives.

Once I was praying over a problem that had been bothering

29

me for a long time. Since I couldn't understand why it had all had to happen I have to admit that I wasted much prayer puzzling over it. One day in the quiet the Lord spoke to me. I understood that I was to cease trying to figure out what had happened. In time I would understand clearly.

Those were not profound words but they were calming. It took almost two years before I understood what had happened, two years when I was able to remind myself not to waste any energy or prayers trying to figure it out.

We need to be quiet before God. A friendship can't be a monologue. We need to talk to him, yes, but just as much we need the conviction, the counsel, the encouragement, the intimacy that comes only when we listen.

Intercession

I used to think that if I couldn't be a George Mueller or a Reece Howell, two men both noted for their intercessory prayer, then I couldn't be an intercessor. Now I know differently. Intercession is not for the great and the few; it is for us all. Everyone of us is called to intercession, to spend time praying for one another (James 5.16).

Before I learned this, the following scenario had happened more than once: I was at the market and I met a friend who asked me to pray for her child. 'Oh, yes', I promised, 'I will.' Because I didn't have a proper prayer time I forgot all about it.

A week later when we met again she exclaimed, 'O Pat, thank you for praying. My little child is so much better now.' There I stood not knowing what to say. Should I admit I'd forgotten? Should I assume credit for time never spent in prayer? I smiled and mumbled and promised myself it would never happen again. And yet it did - until I had a special unhurried prayer time built into my day.

Now when someone says, 'Will you pray for my husband' or 'for this situation', I say 'Yes' and really *do* it. But I've learned not to go rushing into prayer for the answers I think should happen. It's better to spend some time just waiting in the quiet with this person's need before God, so that he can direct the prayers and they can be his will.

My friend Patti Stametts, a woman of much prayer, was asked to intercede for a group of Mafia leaders that had brought all sorts of vice and corruption to a small town. Patti knew the importance of finding God's will first, especially in such a situation as this. After all, how do you pray for the Mafia?

As she waited before the Lord she heard him say in her heart, *'pray for their children.'*

'Their children, Lord? How will that help the situation?' Then she remembered a scripture, *'A little child shall lead them'* (Isaiah 11.6). Of course, good and bad alike love their children and are touched by their innocence. She would pray for the children and the children would lead their parents.

One day my neighbour Barbara asked me to pray about her problem. As I knelt and asked the Lord to show me her need I heard the words, *'she needs somebody with skin on.'* With skin? That seemed such a strange statement yet I understood. At that moment she needed somebody to share her pain.

I got up from my knees and walked across the back yard to her home. We had tea and talked for a long time. I knew it was right for me to be there that day instead of in my prayer corner. To my surprise a week or so later she told me that the day I had come and stayed she had told the Lord that even though his prescence was divine she needed someone with skin on!

I've found that 'praying the Scriptures' for other people is always praying God's will for them. Once a friend confided that a man in Christian leadership was becoming involved with a woman already married. The scripture that came to mind to pray for him was from Colossians. I paraphrased it to fit this man.

> *'Lord, help him to do away with sinful, earthly things: deaden the evil desires lurking within him; help him to have nothing to do with sexual sin, impurity, lust and shameful desires: help him not to worship the good things of life for that is idolatry.'*
> *(Colossians 3.5 paraphrased).*

After many weeks of praying I heard the 'situation' was over. There were others praying, I'm sure, but 'praying the Scriptures' is a powerful way to pray. I remember to pray this one for myself from time to time.

Praying for others is like fighting for them or protecting them. If able, we would certainly protect our friends from physical disasters. One of my sons rescued a baby out of a pool. Another time he rescued his little brother from being swept away by a river.

31

He wanted no thanks; he was there at the needed moment and did what he could. So it is with intercession. When there is time set aside for prayer and a need comes to our attention it is simply a matter of being in the right place at the right time, doing what we can do.

My Needs

Finally, we also need to pray for ourselves. This kind of prayer is not selfish, in fact it says to God, '*I need you. I need your help. I can't do this by myself.*' Admitting our need strengthens our relationship with him. And it strengthens us as well. We are never so strong as when we exchange our weakness for his strength.

Many times I've called on that strength. '*Lord, help me to get through the holidays. Lord, help me to get through just this one day with all these people*' (we had fourteen people living in our house last summer and one of them didn't speak any English!) '*Lord, help me in this burning disappointment. Lord, help me as I confess this sin and failure.*' In every case his strength has replaced my own.

Five Years Later . . .

After five years of tithing my time in prayer, has there been a pay-off? Has the effort been commensurate with the reward? The answer, even in 'human' terms, is 'Yes'.

After one year had gone by Bill asked, 'Would you like to pray with me for an hour each morning?' Bill had spent as little time in prayer as I had previously, so this was a major change for him. Now I have a good early morning start for my prayer time and this prayer together continues to be a great experience for our marriage.

Five years ago our six oldest children were all away from the Lord. Now they are back.

For me there is a new closeness with the Lord, a sense of being perfectly comfortable in his presence. It's like visiting the home of a dear friend. You've been there so often you feel totally at ease. There is no awkwardness, no getting used to the surroundings.

Undoubtedly, there are many needs of many people that change my plans for prayer time. If I don't get back to prayer that day I realise it can't be helped and don't fret. I understand the tithe of time to be a guideline and not an unbending rule.

After five years I have no regrets. Whatever housework has gone undone, whatever part of my career may have been given up, whatever struggles there may have been I do not mind. For I have had instead something very precious; the experience of prayer which cannot be taken away.

3 Anne Townsend:
When God Seems far Away . . .

My last plane flight from Thailand back to England left me breath-less and bewildered. Usually those long hauls by jet were eternities of aching legs, sleeplessness and boredom. But that flight, when I returned to England after sixteen years working in Thailand as an up-country missionary doctor, was different. Before, whatever the physical discomforts, I had sensed an expectancy, a sense of urgency and purpose. I knew that God had something he wanted me to do. On that final flight there was only a dull sense of failure and meaninglessness.

In that plane I was trapped out of time and reality, alone with my thoughts. I tried to pray, but words did not come. God seemed a million miles away. I sank back in my seat, turned on the plane's internal music and listened over the headphones. Suddenly above the crescendo of a Beethoven symphony came familiar Bible words: '*Underneath are the everlasting arms.*' That was all. No feeling, no emotion. Just a statement of fact.

In response to my unspoken prayer, 'Please help me now God!' had come God's words to me: Don't worry. My arms are round you. I'll catch you, and I won't let you down.'

I used to worry when I couldn't sense God's reality. I had been taught that this was because I had acted wrongly, or had an unforgiving attitude toward others. Or perhaps because I was harbouring critical feelings about someone, or had a wrong attitude to God himself. I know that all these things must be brought to the cross of Jesus in repentance and confession before I can enter God's presence. Yes, I have always understood that.

But returning from missionary work in Thailand to life in England has highlighted two other factors involved in being allowed to taste the sweetness of God's presence. First, that some-times there is a blockage in myself that I cannot alter for the time

35

being; and second, that I cannot expect to enter his presence as a right.

In my final few years as a missionary I had begun to discover that emotional upheavals *were* a barrier to sensing God. Nothing was a bigger barrier than a major loss in my life. My ability to feel God's reality disappeared every time I sent my children away to boarding school thousands of miles away in England; when I left my parents, when I was bereaved, and finally when I left sixteen years of life in Thailand.

It was this feeling that I had lost the sense of God's reality that made me understand I could not take pleasure in his presence as my right. At times God gave me the privilege of feeling he was there, at others I began to understand he wanted me to go on trusting him when I felt nothing but emptiness, and prayer was a ritual.

I had to learn that prayer did not depend on whether I felt God's reality or not. God taught me that he is as real when I do not sense him as when I do, and it was returning to England from missionary work that really taught me this lesson, although in a funny way I was learning all over again what I had known all my Christian life.

For years as a Christian I had prayed because I had been taught to do so, and because the Bible told me to. I acted in faith, prayed and trusted that a God was there, who answered my prayers and who heard me. In my early years as a Christian, my Christianity was very much a case of setting my will to be in line with God's will, and acting accordingly. I knew that as I prayed I opened the opportunity for God to show me what his will was, because I was opening myself up to him and to this possibility.

I had been a Christian for about twelve years and a missionary for six when I wrote a book which others appreciated – *Prayer without Pretending*. It was then that prayer took on new dimensions.

It is difficult to capture what happened in mere words, and this is possibly the first time I have even tried to do this.

One day I was sitting alone in my room in our wooden Thai house. I was longing to meet God through the Bible, and I was open to him to say anything he wanted to me when I read his Word. But something totally different happened to me. As I sat there waiting to hear God through the pages of the Bible, I suddenly sensed an overpowering presence in that tiny room.

36

'*God is here with me!*' I told myself. I was caught up in something some might dismiss as a mystical ecstatic experience. But I know that what I experienced was the presence of the living God in my room, by my side. I saw nothing but I felt his reality.

I didn't know how to react to this awesome majestic holy Presence. I didn't know how to bow down and worship. My breath was taken away by a sense of beauty and the reality of the God I could neither see nor touch. When I opened my mouth to speak, I found my mere human words could not convey the depths of worship with which my heart was overflowing. And from my mouth came words I did not know, in a rhythm and melodic pattern that surprised me.

Being allowed to sense God's reality became an integral and important part of my life. The knowledge that Christianity is based on biblical truth is still vital to me, but the joy of being permitted, at times, to sense I am experiencing a foretaste of heaven in the presence of God, is a richness and a sweetness that has enhanced my life as a Christian.

And it was the latter that disappeared when I came back to England after sixteen years of missionary work. Returning to England had been a major upheaval. It wasn't planned. *We* had planned to stay in Thailand as missionaries all our lives. Then one day when my husband, a surgeon, was operating, he heard God's voice directing him in the operating room: '*Go back to England and be a father to your children.*'

In one way I was thrilled, for the mother in me longed never to be separated from my children again. Events in the life of our family confirmed God's call to John to return to England. But it all happened so quickly!

In July I was anticipating another three years in Thailand before our leave, and by mid-September John and I were in England. Everything was moving so fast that I was breathless and unable mentally and emotionally to catch up with the racing weeks that moved us from Thailand to Britain.

We landed in England. Suddenly, I had a sinking feeling that as I was no longer an OMF missionary the mission would not provide for me beyond a limited period. What I was *really* saying was that as I was no longer a missionary, *God* would not provide for me. 'What are we to do?' we asked God, as we waited in a friend's home to sort out our future.

'*Underneath are my everlasting arms*' had been God's word to me on the plane, and I clung on to this.

Prayer at that time was inarticulate trusting. If God was there, I certainly couldn't sense him. If he had a plan for our future, then standing among the shattered heap of bright plans we had cherished I couldn't see what those plans might be. My old identity of missionary doctor no longer existed; what my new role was to, be was still shrouded in mystery. I belonged nowhere. The question hammered away relentlessly in my brain: '*What now*?'

Within five days of being in England John was offered full-time work with Tear Fund. This job was so right that there was no question about it. In the face of the fact that the job fitted John perfectly there was no question of our even visiting a general practice where work was available for us both.

My next potential request, '*God, we need a car*,' was answered before I needed to ask. On arrival in England a friend left a car for us to borrow till we had settled in – and it was there waiting for us at our friend's house when we stepped off the plane.

Bewildered by the sudden changes, I had not asked '*Where do we live, God*?' Suddenly God gave a house in New Malden, with John's job – a house, fully furnished, available to Tear Fund staff.

'*What Church, God*?' was also answered before we asked. Our local church – in which we worshipped that first Sunday – was full of God's children who took to us, strangers as we were, and loved us as part of God's family. All our immediate needs were supplied before I even asked God.

Then John took up his first overseas assignment for Tear Fund and was away frequently working with refugees for our first six months after leaving Thailand.

It was then that I began to pray again – *really* to pray. And it was then that I realised that I could no longer sense the sweetness of God's presence as I had in previous years. And that hurt.

Resting, rejoicing and being refreshed by a sense of God's reality had been strength to me in the past. Now when I felt I most needed it, it seemed denied. And I was too tired to ask why, to be angry, or to do anything other than weep and weep at my sense of loneliness and isolation. I tried to pray, I did ask, I did intercede but I no longer sensed God there in the room with me.

I knew I needed a job. My husband's income was insufficient for us in our mid-forties to be first-time house buyers and to start life in England with nothing in the bank.

'*What am I to do, God*?' My husband was overseas and I vaguely looked for work. There was free-lance writing I could do for Tear Fund, but I needed a regular income if we were to get a mortgage. There was a partnership in General Practice in Wimbledon, but I needed to be at home at nights and weekends with the family to free John for his overseas trips.

When no work came, my prayers changed. '*God, am I a returned missionary such a failure that you haven't any work for me to do in England*?' As I prayed, again I knew that fact had to be stronger than feelings and that God had promised '*underneath are the everlasting arms*'. They held me in those lonely months of trying to fill an unfamiliar and unwanted role of British housewife, and feeling there was nothing for me to do in my new life.

It soon became obvious that we needed to look for a house. The one we rented was ideal for our immediate needs but as our children were leaving boarding school, we needed a bigger home for them.

Homes and schools . . . that was something tangible about which I could pray. The excellent local boys grammar school told me that there was no chance that our sons could be fitted in, as places were taken and it was the wrong time of year anyway. '*God, what now*?' I asked. He answered. Following an interview with the headmaster, I heard that a place was unexpectedly available for our younger son, and our elder could enter the sixth form with no problems.

House prices were mountains my faith was too small to move. While John was overseas I trekked round from agent to agent, from house to house. My faith was like a pricked balloon. Tired, dispirited, I allowed myself to think '*The God who provided for us as missionaries won't provide for us in England. It's up to you, girl, to find somewhere and to do something*.' And that was my big mistake. I grew more and more depressed and hopeless. No way could we ever hope to buy a house.

Then it happened. Geoffrey Maughen, our curate phoned, 'Go and look at a house in Beechcroft Avenue. It's not on the market yet but it will be soon. A church member's mother owns it . . .' I went. I stood in the garden looking at that house and I was angry. Angry with Geoff for not understanding that we could never live in a house as lovely as that one – the price had to be double or treble our hopes of a mortgage. Even more, I was angry at God. Why had he allowed us to slog for him all those years in

Thailand and let us down now when it came to finding somewhere to live in England? Why should my children have to live in a miserable house, when as children of the King of kings they deserved better?

And then I was hit between the eyes. In the dining room of that house was Christ Church New Malden's text for the previous year, hanging on a card on the wall. It said, 'God is able'. Such simple words that my confusion and bitterness rose in tears as I stumbled out of the house into the car.

I drove out of sight and stopped round a corner. 'God, it isn't fair!' I cried. 'I am able!' was the reply. 'Wishful thinking . . . don't delude yourself . . . be realistic . . . face the facts,' my intellect told me.

But, as I started the car again I was cloaked in a feeling so unbelievable that I didn't believe it. I felt that God was going to give us that house.

I had to believe it. A few hours later the owner's son phoned. 'Do you want first option on the house?' I gulped, 'We've no money at all'. 'I didn't ask that,' was the gist of his reply. 'Do you want first option or not? I'll phone back.'

Did we want that house! Yes, yes, a hundred times yes! It was better and lovelier than anything we had looked at in the back-ends of New Malden. This was a house I would choose as a home were I in a position to choose.

'Father, God, You can't give us this, can you?' was my pathetic prayer.

'Watch and see', was his word to my heart.

And a series of extraordinary events started up so that we were able to begin to buy that house. God taught me that he answers my prayers and moves mountains even when my faith is insufficient. He understands my frailty and provides as a loving Father.

With the promise of the house came two offers of work for me – work in writing, which I love. I suppose God had to let me get to rock bottom about a job so that when it came I knew it was from him, and had little to do with my natural gifts and skills. When it came, it was an invitation to work for Buzz Christian Ministries for a trial period – and I'd never read Buzz Magazine before! Then came the offer of the editorship of the new magazine about to be launched, Family Magazine.

The first year of Family Magazine was hard tough work. On

my own, with no secretary or assistant editor for the first few months, I worked early and late and cancelled summer holidays. Prayer was snatched moments of 'Help, God, I can't cope!' And God helped.

Once I had assistance in the office and learned how to run a magazine, life fell into a pattern again. And after a year-and-a-half of praying in the faith that biblical facts *were* true, God allowed me to feel his presence again.

I need times when I can be alone with God and let him speak to me as well as talk to him myself. But prayer is much more a constant affair. For me it must now include bringing God into every situation and every person I meet. 'Lord, Pete looks pale – please help him'. 'Help me to have the right words for that woman on the phone who's lost her baby'. 'How can I get supper for the family when the magazine deadline is running late? Please help!' 'The news about Uganda . . . Father, help me to enter in'. 'I'm so happy to have you here with me in the High Street, Lord. Thank you for being with me. Thank you for the dancing daffodils in the park, and for the miracle of new birth'.

In my life God teaches me different things about prayer at different times. I'll never arrive. I'll never know it all, because the richness of everything God is can never be grasped by my finite mind.

But, '*Thank you God for the joy of prayer, and for teaching me about yourself as I pray!*'

4 Gail Lawther:
Obedience Matters

1982–83 must go down in my personal history as the year I learned to say 'Yes' to God. I have been a Christian since I was seventeen, and it wasn't that my spiritual life had been barren beforehand. In fact, God has slowly been building me up, establishing me in my faith, and teaching me more of himself through good and bad times. But in these months God taught me once and for all that his ways are not our ways, and that our understanding of what is and is not feasible/sensible/ a good idea is not necessarily his!

It began with work. We were living in a council house in East London. I had just left full-time employment and gone freelance, partly to establish myself in work that I could do when we had children, and partly so that I could do more of the embroidery that I had been itching to do professionally. A Christian firm in Worthing were interested in interviewing Chris, my husband, for a job, even though I had confidently assured him that it was no use getting a job in Worthing as it was too far away.

He returned from interview with the offer of a job – and of course I assured him again that he couldn't possibly take it. We couldn't move to Worthing, it would be too far to commute from London, and I couldn't leave all the work contacts I'd been establishing. He phoned up the firm, ostensibly to say 'No', but found himself saying that he would think it over again. I'm not generally given to complaining, but over those next months Chris must have got tired of the sound of my voice saying 'we can't possibly more to Worthing because . . .'.

For five unbelievable months he commuted from Dagenham to Worthing every day, leaving the house at 5.30 am and getting back late at night. We realised that this simply couldn't continue, and so started praying about alternatives. The logical step seemed to be a council house swap to Croydon – near London for my work contacts, and within commuting distance of Worthing for

Chris. Many weeks went by with no news, but eventually we were offered a flat. By this time we had been saying to God, 'No matter how bad it is, we'll take it; we won't be proud or choosy'. We went to see the flat one Saturday; it was a tatty, minute place overlooking a graveyard. Despite our willingness to accept anything – and obviously many people live in far worse accommodation than this – we simply felt no leading from the Lord whatsoever to take up the offer.

We returned home very despondent indeed, and turned to prayer; we kept saying in confusion, 'Lord, what *do* you want us to do? What are you trying to tell us? Where *do* you want us?' Chris mentioned that there was a flat for sale in Worthing just round the corner from his work – was it worth seeing how much they were selling it for? By this time we were desperate, so had nothing to lose. On the Monday evening Chris came home raving about this light, airy flat only five minutes from the sea. I went to see it on the Wednesday; on the Thursday our offer was accepted. Six weeks later we were living in Worthing! Ever since the first day I saw the flat, I have never had a moment's doubt that this is where God wanted us. We didn't even look at any other houses; we fell in love with this one, and the speed with which the normal obstacles in house-buying were overcome confirmed that God had smoothed the way in an amazing and humbling manner. As soon as we had been willing to go where *God* wanted us to go, everything fell into place.

As they say in all the worst novels – little did we realise how much that decision was going to affect our lives. Chris was doing some design work for Colin Reeves of Herald House, Herald House was moving to Worthing, and Colin was thinking of starting up a magazine for Christian women. He was looking for a young, fairly unconventional Christian woman to be editor, with experience relevant to a women's magazine, and decided to interview me.

I went along to the interview knowing what he was going to ask me, if I proved suitable, and determined to say 'No'. I was quite convinced of the need for such a magazine – I had become increasingly sickened with the anti-Christian attitudes promoted by the secular women's magazines, and felt it was high time that Christian women were provided with a positive alternative. I was quite willing to help set up the magazine, but I couldn't edit it;

that would take up too much of the time I wanted to spend on embroidery, and besides, I had just left a full-time editing job.

As Colin talked about his aims for the magazine, I could feel my heart sinking as God showed me that I was the obvious person to undertake the work. I had just the right experience, abilities and attitudes, was just the right age, and was about to move to Worthing. Against all my logical instincts, I agreed to go and talk it over with Chris. I felt that this would be a very good way of testing whether it was God's will. Chris had been totally behind me in my decision to go freelance – in fact I would never have dared do it without his support and encouragement. I was sure that he would feel that I should stick with the craftwork in case I regretted my decision later; on the other hand, I didn't want to take on *Christian Woman* unless Chris was also behind me in this project. In trepidation I rang him to say tentatively that I might agree to the job, and his reply was 'I'm so glad. I didn't want to push you into something you wouldn't be happy doing, but I think you could do this really well.' That banished the last remaining doubts, and I phoned Colin and confirmed that I would be editor for the three trial months we had planned for the magazine – at that time I didn't think any further ahead.

From the very first issue it became obvious that *Christian Woman* was filling a great need and was going to be a success. And this is when my spiritual problems really began. The children that Chris and I dearly wanted had failed to materialise, causing me in particular much distress. I was appalled as the realisation dawned that I was going to have to continue with the magazine – in my mind it seemed that if I said 'yes' to a new career, God would think that I didn't want any children. I would have made a feminist's blood run cold, telling God that I didn't want a career, I wanted to stay at home and have a baby!

It wasn't that I didn't enjoy *Christian Woman* – very far from it. It was, and still is, a very exciting project to be involved in, and I never get bored with it. I also had been able to continue doing embroidery professionally, which gave me added satisfaction. And yet, as every month's issue came out, I would be thinking, 'perhaps I'll be pregnant by next month'. I couldn't make a date in my diary without thinking 'perhaps I'll be pregnant by then'. When I was planning future issues, I would think 'perhaps someone else will be editor by that stage'. I think the magazine is all the stronger because I have had to face up to the challenge anew every month, and really struggle to give myself wholeheartedly to what God has given me to do.

All this time I was fighting my own battle in prayer over our childlessness. Although Chris and I shared a strong desire for children (we both wanted to have at least four), like many men he found it easier to dwell on the compensations of being child-free. The emotional yearning to have children seems to hit women far more strongly; from observing our friends, it seems that the paternal instinct is generally awakened more once the baby is actually conceived or born. So, essentially, it was a battle I fought privately with God.

For many months I thought of it primarily as a problem of guidance; I wanted God to tell me whether we were going to have children, and if so when, and how we would know definitely. It slowly dawned on me that it was actually a problem of suffering – a term I had previously associated only with physical pain. Childlessness was a deep emotional hurt through which God was going to teach me, and us both, a great deal.

Early on in our attempts to have a child I had been very bitter towards God, I felt that he was being very unfair. We had conscientiously built up our marriage relationship and established ourselves in steady jobs, studiously using contraception to avoid conceiving a baby irresponsibly. There we were, waiting for a much-wanted child who failed to appear, while couple after couple among our friends were conceiving babies accidentally. It seemed so cruel. Very slowly I came to the realisation afresh that God does not torment people, that he only works in our lives what is the very best for us. It was no use applying human logic and saying 'why shouldn't I have a baby? It's my right as a woman!' God has pledged to provide everything good and needful for his children, and if I was going to insist on demanding a baby 'or else', I was going to miss out on everything else that he had planned for us.

At one point, when the hurt had become unbearable I broke down and cried and cried before the Lord. I told him that I could just about bear the pain now, but that I simply didn't have enough strength to go through middle age and old age and forever without children. And the Lord showed me that of course I was absolutely right – I haven't got enough strength at the moment. He doesn't require me to be strong enough now to face the whole future: that's one reason he doesn't tell us what the future is going to be.

If we were that strong, we wouldn't need to look to him for his strength as it is needed. There is a song by Second Chapter of Acts which expresses this perfectly: '*I need your hand to guide me every step along the way, I need your arms to hold me; I need your love to fall down fresh upon me every day*'. I've listened to that song many times since, to bolster my failing courage.

I also had to face the problem of getting the whole thing out of proportion, which is the problem of many childless women. Children become the be-all and end-all. I am very blessed by God that I am very happily married indeed. It became important to remember that the prime reason I wanted children was so that we would bring them up together; as James Dobson says in one of his books, a marriage is a complete unit in itself. Children are an added bonus. Many childless couples feel they might as well not continue in their marriage – having children becomes more important than having a fulfilling relationship, and can turn an otherwise very good marriage completely sour. I'm glad God showed me this danger very early on.

There is also the danger, with any kind of suffering or loss, of feeling that all your problems would be solved if only you had this one factor in your life. As well as children, this attitude is also particularly true of many people who lack money, employment, health or a spouse. Even as Christians, we tend to blame all our problems on the one thing wrong in our lives, forgetting that because we are human, things will never be perfect. I realised that I could easily become very ungrateful. Here I was with a very happy marriage, church life and job, with plenty of money and excellent health, and all I could do was complain about the one thing I hadn't got. I realised with a shock that this is what Adam and Eve did; God gave them everything their hearts could desire, but they still wanted the only thing that God said they could not have. Of course something like childlessness still hurts, but God has taught me not to devalue all the good things he has given me. As a result, I find more and more things to praise him for every day.

So, I began to accept in theory that we might not have any children (we were still undergoing tests at this time), but I found it very difficult to open myself fully to what God might want me to do instead. Hints had come from various sources that perhaps I should write a book, but I had spiritually frozen to the spot. I was at the stage of saying 'All right Lord, I can see you don't want me to go in *that* direction, but I just haven't got the courage to step out in any other direction.' Until, that is, we had to miss an evening service at our church. When I asked one of the other members about the sermon, she said 'The message was, that if God has told you to do something, you jolly well get on and do it.' A succinct and very piercing message that reached right into my conscience. The following morning found me on my knees literally and spiritually, saying 'All right Lord, I will do what you want me to do'. I went in to work and found in my post three offers to write books . . . As I opened each of them in turn I became helpless with laughter, once again I was learning how quickly and definitely God moves once you say 'yes' to him.

I remember a talk at the Christian Union when I was at university. The speaker said 'Many of you will be content 'just' to be Christians. Yes, you are saved and have a living knowledge of Jesus Christ, but you will go your own way in the world as much as possible. But some of you will seek night and day to serve God with all your being.' And I prayed that evening that I would be one of those few people. And, through these traumatic months, God has presented both of us with the choice of being 'just' Christians, or giving everything – all our ambitions, rights, hopes and plans – to him. And we have chosen, individually and as a couple, to be wholly his, because nothing else has any meaning in this life. If we don't do his will, then we are standing in his way. We have been challenged on this level in our church life and our own spiritual lives, as well as over the whole question of children. Consequently, we were united in our aims when we received the curt letter from the specialist telling us that we had no hope of ever having children.

It's impossible to explain the mixture of agony and peace that we experienced as we wept in each other's arms for the children that we would never have, and yet at the same time rested in our loving Father's arms, and knew his tender care and guidance. I know now that I want more than anything to do what God wants me to do with my life - yes, more than children, more than marriage to my beloved husband, more than health or strength. I want my life to blossom in the joy and service of the living God.

Now I find that I can sit down and book dates in my diary for months ahead without qualm. As *Christian Woman* has grown, we have been making occasional plans that stretch forward even years, and I'm able to do this with peace. A couple of months ago I was thinking about my work and the fulfillment I get from it, and I suddenly realised that I would have to feel really called by God to leave the magazine. What a transformation: I had to be kicked into it; now I would have to be dragged away from it!

It would be very easy for other childless women to look at my life and say 'It's all right for you not having children, you've got a really exciting job, but I'm just stuck in my everyday life at home or in the office'. If anyone is tempted to say that, I would reply that I only have this job because I have learned, the hard way, to say 'Yes' to God. My life is not the only one that he has exciting and fulfilling plans for – I do not have a monopoly on his loving care. You might feel that God is saying 'No' to you, but are you also saying 'No' to God? If I hadn't learned to say 'Yes' to God, I would be twiddling my thumbs in a council house in Croydon.

5 Caroline Urquhart:
Always Learning

Before I became a Christian, my experience of prayer was confined to the set service in church on Sundays. As a young girl I was in the choir and took my turn pumping the organ, which I much preferred to singing. There were occasions when I found myself shouting to some unknown higher being called 'God'; but only in very difficult situations and certainly without expecting such prayers to be answered.

My main problem was that I didn't know the person to whom I was meant to pray.

That was still my predicament when I married a clergyman. I didn't see any need to pray and had no desire to do so; neither did I seriously believe that I could know this God of whom my husband spoke. But I began to see the effect of prayer in his life and work. Others in the parish prayed and seemed to receive what they asked for. There was no denying that people were being healed physically and emotionally as a result of prayer.

At first I tried to avoid the implications of all this for my own life. However, slowly it dawned on me that prayer could be powerful and was both necessary and important. If it was to be real for me I had to come to know God through Jesus Christ, his Son.

To know Jesus involved handing over my life to him, giving myself to him, acknowledging I could no longer manage my life and relationships alone. It had taken years of internal struggle to reach the point of wanting him to live in me and many weeks of anguish before I finally surrendered myself to him. I gave him my life and he gave me his.

Suddenly I could identify with the words of Jesus: 'On that day you will realise that I am in my Father, and you are in me, and I am in you.' (John 14.20) Now I had a relationship with Jesus and found I could talk to him meaningfully.

51

Looking back, I am sure that initially much of my prayer was selfish. I was concerned about myself and the needs of my family and friends, but at least I knew God was hearing my prayers.

And yet something more was needed if there was to be power when praying about big needs. From seeing the changes taking place in others around me, I knew I had to be baptised in the Holy Spirit, the event promised by Jesus before he returned to be with his Father.

I saw in the book of Acts that some believers in Samaria had accepted the Word of God and had been baptised in the name of Jesus, but had not yet received the Holy Spirit (Acts 8.14–17). Furthermore the apostles went on receiving the Holy Spirit to enable them to do God's will (Acts 4.29). And Jesus had promised that the Spirit would teach us everything we need to know and be our Counsellor.

Even if I had received the Spirit, I had not experienced a release of his power in my life or in my praying. When I was filled with the Spirit I experienced the joy of the Lord as never before and was delighted to discover the words of the Bible coming to life. No longer did they seem dull and dry and aimed at someone else. I found that Jesus was speaking directly to *me*.

This was invaluable as far as my prayer life was concerned. As I prayed for different people and situations, the Holy Spirit often directed me to specific scriptures. Particular verses would be impressed on my mind, sometimes giving clarification about how to pray or what to believe in that situation; at other times indicating how God would answer.

It was helpful to experience the Holy Spirit giving me pictures in my mind that also threw light on a particular need. I suppose I was amazed at the variety of such pictures and how they were always so appropriate. But then I was only beginning to understand how I would have to learn dependence on the Holy Spirit if I was to pray effectively.

I longed for the gift of speaking in tongues, in a language given by God. Before I had given my life to Jesus, hearing people pray in tongues had really bothered me. No doubt that was because I was unable to do it myself. But prayer was fast changing for me and had ceased to be a list of things I was asking God to do.

I *wanted* to praise and worship him. There was now such love in my heart for him that this had to be expressed in some way.

Who but the Holy Spirit would know the best way of worshipping the Father? And we are told to pray at all times 'in the Spirit.'

When I was able to use the gift of tongues, I discovered that although I did not understand what I was saying, I received understanding in my mind. And when I was worshipping God, the Spirit was saying all that I could not find adequate words to express. I found myself singing to him with such love and praise. I could release myself to him in a much deeper and fuller way. This was important for me, as I had always been a rather shy and diffident person.

This is not to imply that everything about prayer was now easy. Certainly I could now pray, but I discovered that Jesus does not separate his teaching on prayer from our need to have faith. The Holy Spirit wanted to supply not only words and pictures to aid my understanding. He wanted to give me real faith in God's promises.

Much of my praying was with others and I found this much easier than praying on my own. When the children were small, it was difficult to maintain concentration when alone with God. I became accustomed to talking to him at odd quiet moments during the day. It was hard to sustain prayer for longer periods of time and, to be frank, I often felt so tired there was usually great temptation to relax and go to sleep instead.

I found the discipline of prayer groups a great help and meeting with other individuals specifically to pray aided concentration and faith. We could learn to agree together as to what we believed God would do in answer to our prayers. Jesus promised: 'Again, I tell you that if two of you on earth agree about anything you ask for, it will be done for you by my Father in heaven. For where two or three come together in my name, there am I with them.' (Matt. 18.19–20)

When we first moved from parish life, I suddenly felt very alone. My husband and the others living with us were often away teaching and preaching and so I had to learn to depend on the Lord myself. At first that was both lonely and difficult. Gradually, however, it became more and more a reality for me that God was my Father.

When Jesus taught his disciples to pray, he told them to begin with the word 'Father'. I discovered everything else followed from that. He is my Father, who loves me and cares for me, who hears me and wants to answer me because I am one of His precious children.

I didn't exactly feel precious. I still felt so unworthy in myself and the enemy often tempted me to think negatively. When I yielded to that temptation it was difficult to pray at all, let alone have faith. But slowly I came to understand that I had been made acceptable to God through the precious blood of Jesus that cleansed me of my unworthiness. I could approach him as my Father, confident of his love.

But I had to learn how to deal with the negative, unbelieving thoughts that plagued me.

When Jesus taught his disciples to pray with faith, he told them to have faith in God. That seems so obvious. But I realised that often I was believing the size of the problem or difficulty rather than the bigness of God. Certainly there were times when I believed my negative feelings and fears instead of his words.

Jesus then told them: 'I tell you the truth, if anyone says to this mountain, 'Go, throw yourself into the sea,' and does not doubt in his heart but believes that what he says will happen, it will be done for him.' (Mark 11.23) I had heard of mountain-moving faith but I knew I had to learn on the mole-hills!

I began by rebuking the symptoms of a cold, refusing to accept the headache and sore-throat and telling them to go in the name of Jesus. Neither were they to return or affect anyone else.

Next I thanked the Lord for my complete healing, for Jesus had continued his teaching by saying: 'Therefore I tell you, whatever you ask for in prayer, believe that you have received it, and it will be yours.' (v.24)

During that day I continually reminded the symptoms they had no place in my body which is a temple of the Holy Spirit. I refused to receive them. Imagine my joy when, by the end of the day, there were no signs of the cold at all. Instead of several days of misery, there had been just one day of battling!

It seems a small matter now, but it did much to boost my confidence at the time. I had participated in faith battles with others, but this was something personal.

Some things did not receive such speedy answers. My son had suffered from eczema since babyhood. Much of his skin was affected and it was heart-breaking to have to bandage his legs and try to stop him scratching. I wanted to fight a similar prayer battle for him, but it seemed as the years passed that God was using this to teach Clive how to hold on to his promise with faith.

It seemed such a hard way for a young lad to learn. He was an anxious child and times of stress made the excema worse. The Lord gave my husband a promise that our son would receive his healing when he was fourteen. Many times we wanted to hasten his healing as we prayed. But God knows his business. He wanted not only to remove the eczema, but to heal the cause of nervousness as well – and teach him to pray with faith.

These things have now happened. Clive began to lose signs of the eczema at fourteen and within months his skin was virtually normal. Certainly, he is not the anxious person he used to be and has a real faith of his own.

And I learned a great deal myself about persisting in prayer, continuing to stand in faith against the disease. If my cold had been a mole-hill, this had been a mountain and God had moved it.

During those years I had experienced many miraculous answers to prayer, both with others in our fellowship and on my own. And yet at no time did I ever feel I was any good at prayer. I was far more conscious of failure with such a need so close to home, and had to go on standing firm against negative thoughts and doubts.

Besides, there were situations which God used to stretch our faith. I was learning that it was not only what I said during the time of prayer that mattered, but my attitude at other times; they indicated where my faith truly was.

As the work of the fellowship expanded so did the need of financial provision. We never raised money, nor did we ask others for it. God taught us that he is our Provider and that if we are seeking to put the work of his Kingdom first and to live in a right relationship with him and with one another, then he will supply for all our needs.

The story of the past few years has been one of remarkable provision. The Lord has supplied the properties we have needed, first a house for the community, a farm where many needy people could receive help, an old cinema as an outreach centre, and recently a college costing well over half a million pounds, where people could be trained for full-time Christian work.

Of course, I have only been one of many praying in faith for these properties and for God to supply the right people to be with

55

us in our work for him. However, it would have been irresponsible to sit back and rely on the faith of others around me. There have been times when I needed to be before God in prayer, confessing the sin of my unbelief and asking him to give me the necessary faith.

On such occasions, the Lord has used the opportunity to sort out many things within my life. You cannot seek the Lord seriously without him shining his light into dark areas of sin and disobedience. It becomes important not only to be in a right relationship with him but with others as well. Jesus said: 'And when you stand praying, if you hold anything against anyone, forgive him, so that your Father in heaven may forgive you your sins.' (Mark 11.25)

And so I have learned that if we are to agree together in prayer, our lives need to be in harmony as well. Living in community means there are plenty of opportunities to forgive others and to be forgiven. Any tensions must be faced and dealt with so we can be in real unity as we come to our Father in prayer.

Satan tries to create disharmony among Christians because he knows this can rob them of effectiveness in prayer. I used not to believe in a personal devil, but I have come, not only to recognise the reality of his existence, but also to exercise the authority over him and his forces that we are given as those who belong to the Kingdom of God. Our prayers can appear to be ineffective at times because we have not undertaken the spiritual battle necessary if we are to see victory in the situation. Our fight is not against people but against the powers of darkness that often bind them, oppress them and create or magnify their problems.

We can fight from a victorious position because Jesus Christ has already won the battle over the forces of evil on the cross. Jesus describes Satan as a liar, a thief and deceiver. He is not to be allowed to deprive us of the freedom we have been given in Christ. Jesus took all our sin, infirmities and grief to the cross so that we might be set free from them.

However, we need to believe in his victory, come to him personally in prayer and appropriate that victory in our own lives and on behalf of others for whom we pray. This involves taking prayer seriously and not giving up until we sense we are in a place of victory. Whatever we bind on earth is already bound in heaven; what we loose on earth is already loosed in heaven. (Matt. 18.18)

There has been so much to learn and yet I feel I know nothing,

56

that I have hardly begun. We live in a world full of need, of desperate and despairing people – facing a lost eternity unless they meet with Jesus. I had to ask him to give me a genuine heart-felt compassion for those who did not know God so that I could pray meaningfully for them. Even so my prayers seem so insignificant against such immense need.

It has been encouraging to be part of a fellowship devoted to praying for a spiritual revival in this country; to be with others who want God to use their lives to extend his Kingdom. We constantly need to experience revival in our own lives if he is going to use us effectively in such work. We need regular times of seeking God in prayer; aiming to draw closer to him and to experience a new spiritual break-through in our lives.

Such times are always rewarding, even though they can be demanding. They are worth it, not only because of the personal benefits, but because we see the increased fruitfulness in the work we do for God. And yet there is never room for complacency or self-satisfaction.

Seeing people come to the Lord, being filled with the Holy Spirit and healed is not enough when so many are left untouched by the good news of Jesus. Constantly I feel challenged by questions the Lord asks us: 'Do you want to be holy? Do you want to be like Jesus?'

Part of me wants to say 'Yes' to such questions; yet there always seems to be another part that wants to shrink away from the implications of following Jesus along the Way of Holiness, about which Isaiah speaks. (Chapter 35) I know I cannot avoid the issue, but there always seems to be so much more breaking to be done in my life so that there is less of me and more of Jesus.

The wonder is that he does love us and continues to change us from one degree of glory to another. He hears our prayers despite all our short-comings and answers us by his grace and mercy.

That does not mean I can ever take my sin and failure lightly. It is serious because it prevents Jesus from doing fully in me all that he wants to do. But I know that whenever I humble myself before him, concentrating on his goodness rather than my imperfections, his hands can really be moved through prayer. He loves honesty and truthfulness.

And we have found as a fellowship that when we meet with God in his holiness, prayer becomes more powerful and natural.

It is no longer a struggle to pray and easier to pray through to victory.

Now I want to learn to live in the holiness of the Lord with his spirit of prayer on me, without slipping back to negative, self-dependent attitudes. Perhaps that seems a forlorn hope. But with God nothing is impossible – for me or for you.

6 Christine Wood:
Links in my Life-line

I learned to pray at my mother's knee. I am grateful that, although not a praying person herself, she taught me to say this simple bedtime prayer:

> *'Gentle Jesus, meek and mild,*
> *Look upon a little child;*
> *Pity my simplicity,*
> *Suffer me to come to thee.'*

That was my nightly talk to Jesus before falling asleep. I believed that he heard and it comforted me to know that he was there, listening, even though I could not see him. Those few words formed the first link in a chain of prayer that has been a vital part of my life ever since.

At seven I attended a school where religious education was taken seriously and Bible teaching formed an important part of my education. I learned that heaven was a completely happy place where Jesus lived. Deep within my heart I longed that he would one day allow me to come to him. How wonderful if he would share that heavenly home with me! And so the words 'suffer me to come to thee' became more meaningful.

At ten years of age I was an adventurous 'loner' and one of my favourite haunts was a hillside thick with hawthorn bushes. I knew most of the tracks through this undergrowth, but one showery spring day I came to a clearing previously undiscovered. Here a few gnarled trees lifted their branches towards the light.

I climbed into one of these trees and sat among the wet branches to delight in the scent of delicate pink blossom. The sun shone briefly on the raindrops and, to my enchanted eyes, they instantly became a myriad of diamonds sparkling on the leaves.

'It's lovely, Jesus!' I exclaimed in ecstasy.

There was nothing pious about my enjoyment of beauty. Those words were a spontaneous appreciation of what I could smell and see. So another link was forged in my prayer chain, a link in which a growing spiritual awareness whispered that God had a hand in the beauty that delighted me. That awareness made me grateful, and it spilled out in the first few words that weaned me from the 'set prayer' learned in infancy. I praised God for the first time.

This inner awareness continued to develop and I knew I had a heavenly Father to whom I could speak freely. The trouble was that my life was so full of other things that I neglected speaking to him with the regularity of my 'Gentle Jesus' days.

The Girl Guides occupied some of my time. Among other activities, a group of us visited an Old People's Home where, one Christmas, we acted a short Nativity play. I was one of the Wise Men, a part which fortunately did not involve much acting. All I had to do was follow the star and try to look reverent about it.

One frail, silver-haired lady, who had become my favourite on past visits, clasped my hands after the Nativity play and said, 'Keep your eyes on that star, my dear. Follow it always.'

Her earnestness puzzled me as we left. I intended to ask her what she meant, but I never saw that elderly friend again as she died before my New Year visit.

On learning of her death, I stumbled from the Home blinded by tears, and darkness fell as I walked slowly away. Several times I paused to gaze up into the dark, velvety sky – remembering what that silver-haired lady had said.

The stars, twinkling in their endless background, filled me with awe and wonder. My friend had told me to follow just one star – but how? Of course that was what the Wise Men did long ago, but then theirs was a special star sent to guide them to Bethlehem. What had it to do with me? I lingered by a gate and took a deep breath of the crisp evening air.

'Please, God, how can I follow a star?' I asked, and continued to gaze upwards while waiting for an answer, since an answer I must have.

After a while a wonderful thing happened. God drew close to me, and I drew close to him – by a gate on a starry night. And there he gave me the understanding for which I yearned. Those Wise Men had followed a star of faith and hope, and it had led them to Jesus. My elderly friend had also kept her eyes on such a star, and she had followed it all the way home to him.

Enlightenment overwhelmed me with awe, utter amazement that the great God who made the stars, also cared about me. That night I learned that communion with God meant listening to his still, small voice, as well as speaking to him. It also involved worshipping him. And so my prayer chain grew by two vital links which I am still exploring.

I entered my teenage years with a conviction that being aware of God was not enough. His greatness, and my appreciation of it, must affect my whole life and outlook.

Just as Saul of Tarsus was never the same again after his encounter with Jesus on the Damascus Road, so my experience of God through prayer and Bible reading (yes, by then I read a few verses daily) must affect the person that I was. It should produce a change.

If I truly wanted to know God more intimately, then Saul's cry on the Damascus road: '*Lord, what will you have me do*?' must become my prayer too, since true worship should motivate me to seek God's will for my life, instead of going my own way.

Although recognising this important fact, many of my prayers were of the demanding type and the petition, 'Give me . . .' was uttered far too often.

In his wisdom, God said 'No' to many of those requests, and 'Wait' to many more. I am grateful that the early links in my 'prayer chain' were gently forged and that God bore with my demands so lovingly. Later I found that other links would be forged in the scorching fires of trial and heartbreak, links that I would gladly have done without but links which the same loving God knew were vital to my spiritual well-being.

Like most girls, my growing-up wants included a husband and for several years God's answer to that prayer was 'Wait'. I went on waiting until Geoffrey stepped into my life.

Once we were married, my prayer life took on new dimensions. It deepened and widened into the precious fellowship of the two of us uniting together to bring God our worship, thanks and requests. And because we weren't perfect we also knelt before him together to plead his forgiveness when we were guilty of wrong thoughts, words, or deeds.

Geoffrey had not long been a Christian when we married and I recall his awe on reading John Wesley's words: '*God does nothing but in answer to prayer'.* As we thought about that together we found it a humbling statement. With legions of angels at his command, God waited for people like us to pray! He chose not to work independently of us. We were amazed.

We also saw the importance of keeping in touch with him as Abraham of old had done, so that we might know his plans. In Genesis the Lord said: *'Shall I hide from Abraham what I am about to do?'* He involved Abraham in his proposed destruction of Sodom. Dismay filled Abraham and he interceded for the wicked city where his nephew Lot lived.

Abraham pleaded with God to spare Sodom if fifty righteous should be found there. The Lord agreed to save the city for fifty's sake. In subsequent prayers Abraham kept lowering the number until he came down to ten righteous, and God agreed not to destroy Sodom for the ten's sake. Abraham stopped praying at this point, with the uneasy knowledge that Lot's family numbered only four.

God did destroy Sodom, but *he remembered Abraham* and brought Lot out of the catastrophe. That man owed his life to his praying uncle. Abraham's prayers taught Geoffrey and me to go on praying, that we also might prevail with God.

When we had been married for seven years, Geoffrey and I enjoyed a delightful holiday in Devon. On the last evening we stood on the balcony of our holiday flat to watch the sea deepen from liquid amber to blood red. It was a beautiful sight, yet a strange melancholy gripped me as we watched. Geoffrey must have sensed my mood, for he put his arms round me, strong and comforting.

'It makes me feel sad to see the sun go down,' I whispered.

'Why should it? It's only moving towards tomorrow,' Geoffrey replied.

Was it the cool evening air, or did some inner sense of forboding make me shiver as we went indoors?

Back home, we went to a friend's house after the evening church service. This friend invited me to speak for a few minutes on my favourite Bible character. I chose Joseph and briefly related the story, again in Genesis, of how his jealous brothers sold him as a slave to passing traders.

Joseph had good cause to hate those brothers, yet when famine eventually re-united them in Egypt, he showed a lovely spirit of forgiveness. *'Do not be grieved or angry with yourselves . . . for*

God sent me before you to preserve life . . . You meant evil against me, but God meant it for good . . .' (Genesis 45.5; 50.20).

I reminded the group present that we all have to face trials of one kind or another. People treat us badly or let us down. None of us know what tomorrow will bring, but God is concerned with our reactions to life's knocks. If someone wrongs us, will we have Joseph's forgiving spirit? What if grief or tragedy strike? Will we cry: 'Why me?' in aggrieved tones, or face our crisis with courage and fortitude? We can either go through it with God's help, showing Joseph's gracious spirit, or we can become vindictive, rebellious and resentful.

As I spoke I little dreamed how soon or how severely I would be tested myself. Two days later Geoffrey went into hospital to have an ingrown tooth removed. I never saw him again! The hospital matron telephoned to tell me that Geoffrey had died under the anaesthetic.

The telephone slipped from my grasp and I stared unseeing out of my office window. Surely, there must be some mistake. My husband was young and fit and, anyway, tragedies like that happened only to other people. Slowly, the dreadful truth dawned and horror changed to grief.

An office colleague drove me to the hospital where the matron brought me Geoffrey's clothes, his watch, his ring. I signed a form, choked down a cup of tea, and my friend drove me home.

Amid the heartbreak and shock, an inner voice reminded me of my recent words: *'What if grief or tragedy strike?'* They had struck, but could I display Joseph's lovely spirit, or would I be bitter and resentful towards God? How could I pray?

Years before I had learned that communion with God meant listening as well as speaking. I listened in anguish and God brought some words from the book of Joshua to my remembrance: *'I will be with you, I will not fail you or forsake you . . . Be strong and courageous.'*

Those words embedded themselves into my heart and mind. There was no escaping them. *'Have not I commanded you? Be strong and courageous! Do not tremble or be dismayed, for the Lord your God is with you wherever you go.'*

I needed such words to lean on and act upon., but that was easier said than done. Shortly after Geoffrey's funeral I was too distressed to pray and could only lie sleepless all night, with a throbbing head.

When at last I did cry out to God, the same words repeated themselves, almost as if they were spoken aloud: '*Have not I commanded you? Be strong and courageous . . .*' In my anguish I did not want to listen, so I put my fingers in my ears to try and blot out this insistent command. By dawn I was exhausted and tears flowed. I felt angry with God. It hurt that he had nothing else to say when I was in such a plight.

That morning the postman delivered many letters, but only one mattered. Geoffrey's brother had sent it and I opened it first. Michael was an army captain and expected his orders to be obeyed. 'Have courage, Christine. Be steadfast,' he had written. That was all.

After reading Michael's note I came to the end of myself. Hadn't I battled with God over those very words all night, telling him that they were of no use, that they failed to meet my need? Still, he would not let me escape from them. Falling on my knees, I admitted defeat.

'Look, Lord, I am afraid,' I prayed. 'When I think of the lonely future it really scares me. I'm not strong either, and, dear God, you've only to look at me to see I'm desperately dismayed. Why keep saying the same thing to me?'

I reached for my Bible, and some inner compulsion made me turn to the very verses I dreaded, almost hated. All in a flash, realisation burst upon me. I had not listened properly nor heard completely. Now the full message leaped from the page, '*I will be with you; I will not fail you or forsake you.*'

How blind I had been! I was so full of what I had to do to cope with the crisis that I had failed to give God a chance. He wanted to take away my fear and make me strong, but I had refused to allow it. He wanted to comfort, but I was too immersed in self-pity for him to get through. All night he had tried to tell me: '*I'm here, I'm holding you and will never let you go,*' but I hadn't listened.

At last I turned to God in repentance, handing myself over to him - grief, fright, weakness and all. A warm, assuring glow flowed through me as his peace, love and power enfolded me. In that moment of reassurance and forgiveness I knew, not only that Geoffrey had gone to be with him, but that God was also close and would never leave me.

In the following days I found that the apostle Paul, who survived many a crisis, had written some powerful words of encouragement: '*I have become absolutely convinced that neither death nor life, neither messenger of heaven nor monarch of earth, neither what happens today nor what may happen tomorrow . . . has any power to separate us from the love of God in Christ Jesus our Lord.*' (Romans 8. 38–39 JBP.)

As I prayed to him with renewed strength and trust, the same loving God saw me through my crisis and many new, strong links were forged in the prayer chain that bound me to him.

Did I learn all that there is to know about prayer in that tragedy? Of course not. Only recently God had something new to teach me, when I was tempted to cancel a teaching engagement at an American writing school. I felt unwell, had an abcessed tooth, and depression engulfed me. Only the thought of the people I would be letting down stopped me from cancelling. Then, shortly before my departure, a friend telephoned.

'You are on my heart, Christine. Have you a burden?' she asked, and I poured out my troubles.

'You are depressed because you are looking within,' my friend said. 'Look up, and praise God! He wants to give you a garment of praise instead of that spirit of heaviness, but you have to look up and take it from him.'

'Praising God is the last thing I feel like,' I complained.

'Well praise him anyway,' Mrs Walton urged. 'And what about God's promises? Aren't you claiming those either?'

To my shame I confessed that I was not.

'Here's one for you to claim right now,' my friend said. '*They that wait upon the Lord shall renew their strength; they shall mount up with wings as eagles; they shall run, and not be weary; and they shall walk; and not faint.*'

Thanks to Mrs Walton's encouragement, I did look up instead of staring at the mire of despondency into which I had sunk. As I praised God and entrusted myself to his keeping, fears and doubts departed and my faith became wonderfully renewed and strengthened.

Once I waited prayerfully on him, God proved faithful to his promise in Isaiah 40. Spiritually I did soar as on eagles' wings and my heart remained at peace as the plane carried me over the Atlantic.

Praise rose to my lips again as that plane touched down in Minneapolis and I thanked God for lifting me out of myself. Sunshine flooded through the opened plane doors and joy flooded

65

my heart. I felt certain that a wealth of spiritual blessing and new experience awaited me out there in the Minnesota sunshine, and so it proved. When, at the end of the course, the students hugged me for coming so far to teach them, my cup of joy overflowed.

Once I fulfilled the condition, God kept his promise, and in so doing he opened up a whole new realm of prayer to me. He taught me to claim his promises. They were in the Bible for me, his child, but I had failed to avail myself of them.

Now, back in the humdrum of everyday living, I still feel a warm glow whenever I recall that soaring experience. Although I do not soar daily in the same way, that promise in Isaiah remains precious as I 'run' in my eagerness to serve God in new ways.

And when not running, I walk without fainting while going about my household tasks. Only this morning a prayer of praise rose to my lips while washing the breakfast dishes:

'Lord, I thank you for the day you taught me to soar on the wings of your promise, and I praise you that, as I press on in the Christian life, there will always be more promises to claim, more times to wait upon you, more to learn about prayer and more opportunities to rejoice in your faithfulness.'

I have linked my progress in prayer to links in a chain, but that chain is no fetter. It is my sure anchor against the storms of life. And that is not all. For me prayer is a lifeline to Eternity.

7 Jean Raddon:
My Hand in His

To write about prayer is not easy, for I am only beginning to understand the heights and depths of this wonderful gift of God. However, I can look back over my life and thank him for teaching me a little of what prayer means – leading me into that lovely relationship of walking with him, where everything that is part of me is shared with him. Walking through the street and seeing a particularly beautiful garden calls out the response in me, 'Oh, Father, isn't it wonderful!' Facing some woman in desperate need, my heart is crying out, 'Help her, Lord!' When someone's name comes into my mind, I immediately tell the Father something about that person, and ask for help for him or her. This relationship is, however, only one aspect of prayer, and it did not happen overnight. It has taken over forty years to develop and even now, I know that there is so much more to be discovered.

I have been helped to understand more about prayer by books of all sorts. Professor Hallesby's book, *Prayer* taught me to search my heart about the hindrances to prayer in my life. I was startled when I first read it to realise that it is possible to hold things in my life which will certainly hinder God's ability to answer my prayers. But it is true. The Bible tells me clearly that if I regard sin in my heart God cannot hear me (Psalm 66.18). This calls for constant discipline in my spiritual life. I have to keep short accounts with God. By his grace when the Holy Spirit makes me aware of sin in my life I must take hold of the forgiveness he offers me. This seems to be a constant thing and as I start each day the cry of my heart is, '*Search me, O God, and know my heart . . . and see if there be any wicked way in me*' (Psalm 139.23). He does this with loving precision and claiming his forgiveness I take courage and press on.

Over the years an increasing conviction has come to my heart about resentment, unforgiveness and bitterness. How very easy it

67

is to let this sort of thing spoil my relationship with him and with others! Many years ago I held a deep resentment against a fellow missionary. It began to intrude into every time of prayer I had. Reluctant to admit that I was wrong in holding this resentment, whether the cause was justified or not, I suddenly found prayer, Bible reading and even fellowship with other missionaries were losing all their joy and power. When, by his grace, I was able to put that situation right then suddenly I was released into a new freedom in all aspects of my Christian life, including prayer.

It was my privilege to be one of the first team of Christian workers to enter the beautiful land of Nepal. There was no church there. No one was allowed to change his religion and no proselytising was allowed. As we started to plan for the beginning of our work there, we looked back over sixteen years of waiting, praying and believing that God would make it possible for us to serve him in Nepal. The year we were able to go in was one of great anticipation. We had a night of prayer, just six women on the roof top of a house in India. As we prayed we suddenly felt the assurance of his answer and our prayer turned to praise as we worshipped him for what he was going to do. Those sixteen years of praying and believing may have seemed like waiting time for us, but the Holy Spirit was able to get to work on human hearts long before we got there in person. As we entered the land we kept meeting people who were very conscious of their need and who were really seeking the living God. So many seemed so easy to talk to and were well prepared by the Holy Spirit to hear his Word. And it was not just our prayers that had helped to bring this about. On my first visit to Australia I met a woman in Melbourne who seemed very excited about all that was happening in Nepal. Forty years before she and her husband had started a prayer group for its people. All those who were in that group had died, including her husband. She had had no idea that the country was open to the Gospel and certainly those who had died never knew. How thrilled I was as I realised afresh this power of prayer to reach into areas that appear to be completely closed – the reality of the church in this land where it all seemed impossible, is living proof that God works in his perfect time, in answer to our prayers.

I can say this with absolute assurance, and yet in spite of that there is so much about prayer, and the way in which God answers, that puzzles me still. Why do some prayers seem to be answered (and I say 'seem' because we shall not know everything until Jesus comes) and some prayers, prayed just as believingly and fervently have no apparent effect, or one very different from what we had hoped for?

A little girl was carried into our dispensary in Nepal. She had fallen out of a tree and torn the artery in her wrist. Almost dead from loss of blood, she had been carried by her parents, who literally ran for three days to get to us. We were nurses, not doctors, but we knew we had to do something. Gingerly I lifted the pad they had placed on the wound and the blood immediately spurted. I hastily put it back. We prayed together, gave her a whiff of anaesthetic and opened up the wrist looking for the bleeding point. The tiny little wrist seemed to me like a nightmare. I could not find the bleeding point. In desperation, worried about letting the child in her weakened state have too much anaesthetic, I said to my colleague, 'I can't do it.' She said quietly, 'Stop panicking. Let's pray.' She prayed asking the Father to do a miracle. I took the tourniquet off, the bleeding had stopped, the arm healed completely in a few days. Prayer was answered.

A lovely young Nepali friend of ours was dying. A cholera-like disease had taken hold of her and we just did not seem to be able to stop the terrible diarrhoea and vomiting. We felt that God could heal her. In fact, we thought of these verses in James 5.14–16, where it says that if one is sick one should call for the elders of the church and they should anoint with oil, pray over the sick one with faith, and healing would take place. So, after careful thought we did just what the Word said. The Pastor and elders came. With joy and hearts full of faith we gathered round the bed. There seemed to be a real sense of God's presence as the Pastor prayed. Ten minutes later the girl was dead. Had prayer been answered?

The woman talking to me was sad. Her fifteen year-old only daughter was dying of leukaemia. Did I think that God could heal her? With a heart full of love for her and her husband I told her that I knew he could and that she and her husband should pray for his will in it all and I would pray with them. A beautiful letter came two years later. '*Dear Miss Raddon*', the mother wrote, '*you will rejoice with us that God has completely healed our lovely daughter. He has taken her to be with himself*'. She went on to say how beautifully God had developed their relationship with himself in those two years and at that point I was reminded again that prayer is primarily a deepening process of our personal relationship with him, whatever the answer. If I trust him when I seem to be up against a brick wall and when the heavens seem as brass, then I suddenly find my personal relationship with him becoming more and more real. I find I am driven to his Word and increasingly I realise that, 'I don't understand but he *is* there, he *is* in control, his Word *does* stand and he *does* love me.' The alternative to this is to let doubt and bitterness take over, resulting in decreasing faith and decreasing desire to read the Word and live by it.

To look at Jesus' life from the perspective of prayer has helped me tremendously. Jesus had this relationship with his Father where he turned everything over to him. He also experienced the 'apparently unanswered' prayer. I say *apparently* unanswered prayer because I do not think there is such a thing. All prayer stems from prompting by the Holy Spirit, and the secret of its effectiveness flows out of our seeking that, '*Not my will, but yours be done*' (Luke 21.42). I am helped as I realise how Jesus must have prayed and agonised over Judas Iscariot. He shares with me the hurt and sorrow over one of his own intimate circle apparently refusing all God's pleadings and going out into an eternity without God. It comforts me, as I pray (and have done for years) for unsaved relatives and friends, that my Lord and Saviour has walked this path with me. There also was his prayer for Peter that Peter's faith would not fail. It seems to point to the time of the denials, but Jesus was maybe looking beyond that to the ultimate answer when Peter would die for his faith.

I was converted from a non-Christian, although very happy, background. I did not realise that I had an uncle, my father's brother, who loved the Lord with all his heart. When I came to know Christ someone told me I should write and tell him. I was delighted to have a visit from him, and with tears in his eyes he told me he had prayed for me every day since I was born. How that has encouraged me both to pray for other members of my family and also to encourage parents to realise that they can be constantly in touch with their children, wherever they are through prayer. I always find in this incident a great incentive to keep on praying.

A greater realisation of the warfare we are involved in has also spurred me on to prayer continually. I am sure that prayer is one of God's mightiest weapons against the enemy that we fight. To accept the reality of Satan and his emissaries is important. So many do not seem to realise what a devilish business we are caught up in when we openly stand on the words of Jesus Christ, '*I am the way, the truth and the life*' (John 14.6). The reality of evil spirits is certainly experienced when one lives in countries where there is no Christian heritage and where Satan has enjoyed complete control for centuries. This is where I really learnt the power of praise in prayer. 2 Chronicles 20 reads, '*when they began to sing and to praise, the Lord set ambushments against the enemy.*' I see more and more situations occurring in life that are, humanly speaking, impossible to cope with. I really do not know why these things have happened or happen – that is, presuming they are not caused by my own sinful disobedience. But suddenly I realised that he knows. He can see the end from the beginning and so I start to praise him. It was when the Israelites began to praise that God moved against the enemy. So I am learning in prayer to praise. I walk about the house with the hymn book, singing his praises. I take the psalms of praise on bended knee and worship him. When I cannot see him working I praise him and worship him because I know he is there and at work. This is specially so where I have unsaved people I love, have prayed for them for many years but there seems to be no move from God. Not knowing what is holding them back, I begin to praise him and it warms my own heart, fills me with assurance that he is working and allows him to move into the situation. He does not always move in the way I would like him to but he does work.

One rather dramatic instance of this was when we had an unpaid account on the mission field. We were sorely puzzled as we had always been able to pay our accounts. This was a large bill of two thousand pounds so we all met together and started to pray. After some time of quietly praying over the whole situation, seeking our own hearts for hidden disobedience, we were suddenly assured that the prayer was answered and we started to praise him for his goodness. We then dispersed to our usual occupations. We did not know where the money was coming from. Mail came in twice a week and we had already had it but we knew the outgoing mail the next morning should have the cheque in it. Then a visitor was seen walking up the path. I sighed and thought of all I had to do, but welcomed her, showing her the hospital and compound, all of which she enjoyed. Then, feeling rather guilty about my unwelcoming heart, even though I had a welcoming smile, I offered to walk to the air strip with her. As this was about three miles away it was a good walk. As we walked she said how impressed she was with the work we were doing and handed me a cheque. I tucked it into my uniform pocket, saw her on to the plane and hurried back to the hospital.

As we met for prayer that evening we wondered why the money promised by our Father had not come. Suddenly I remembered the cheque and in spite of our praise and in spite of our prayer we were surprised when the cheque was for two thousand pounds. That was lovely, but why did he not send the money before that? Why wait until the last moment? I see he often uses these extremities to drive me to him in prayer and praise. Perhaps without that element of testing I would forget him and take all for granted, not keeping up that lovely relationship. It is over-whelming to realise he wants the relationship as well.

I have learned also the wonder of getting hold of God's promises and claiming them when everything seems to be going wrong. Prayer, for me, is a holding on to what God has said to me. This has meant a real battle in prayer as doubts and fears continually arise and I have to go back to his Word in faith. It has been this Word that has comforted me when, seemingly, prayer has not been answered.

For many years I prayed for a brother whose life ended very tragically with a strong possibility of its having been suicide. I was shocked when I heard the news. I could not believe that this man had not come into faith before he died. I immediately went to the Word. Reading the passage from *Daily Light*, a little devotional book, for that evening, it seemed that these words jumped out: '*I have ransomed them from the power of the grave.*' (Hosea 13.14) I still have waves of doubt but every time they come I say to my Father, '*Thank you for that promise. I saw nothing in his life to make me believe it but I believe your Word.*' It always brings peace to my soul. Paul said in one of his letters that we should bring everything to the Father in prayer with thankfulness and then his peace will guard our hearts (Philippians 4.6–7). Paul does not say that every prayer will be answered in the way we think it should. He must have known plenty of apparently unanswered prayer, but giving the situation continually to the Father brings a peace that one just does not understand. It comes I suppose because one realises that the Father is in control.

Many years ago I was helped by Phillips' translation of Romans

8.26: '*We do not know how to pray worthily as sons of God but his Spirit within us is actually praying for us those agonising longings which never find words.*' I realised the wonderful fact that the continuous ache and longing in my heart over people I love, situations I faced and seemingly unsolved problems, was the gracious Holy Spirit wondrously praying through me. Words so often seem so inadequate to express the ache and sorrow in my heart, but the Spirit brings this to the Father in the words which I cannot express. This has strengthened me over the years.

I have found many difficulties in walking the way of prayer and still do. But I am comforted by the feeling, increasing as the years go by, that the Father loves me. He knows that weak and feeble as my love is, I love him. Difficulties must not be allowed to daunt me. Paul said that, though handicapped on every side he was never frustrated. I must never lose my confidence in God who has filled his book with promises I can really hold on to. Discouragement so often seems to take a grip. The only remedy I find for this is to meditate resolutely on him and his Word.

Boredom also has to be grappled with, dreadful as this seems to write. Many Christian writers have experienced this and call it dryness. One of the saints wrote long ago, '*My heart is dried up like a land without water, I find no savour in the psalms, I have no pleasure in reading good books, I am lazy in my work, sleepy in my meditation, . . .*' To quietly persist in prayer, standing against the feelings that do so easily beset me, is the best answer to this for me.

Distractions can also be a problem. It seems incredible that while talking to my heavenly Father suddenly my mind is filled with thoughts of whether the dinner is cooking properly, or whether my car needs to be serviced! I find quiet discipline brings me back to him. Meditation on the fact that he knew something about the pressures of ordinary everyday life in his years in the carpenter's shop continues to help me. Dare I think that he had distractions as he talked with his Father? I do not know, but I know that in every point where I am tempted he was tempted. So his understanding of me is perfect and I press on. When these distracting thoughts come, I turn at once to praise and thanksgiving. This helps tremendously.

Busyness is another distraction. Too much to do and not enough time to do it. Discipline is the answer here. I find that if I do not have my time of prayer early in the day then I do not have it. I

realise people do not always find this the best time. Temperament-
ally I find I am ready for anything directly after I wake up. I have
a friend who takes two or three hours to get going so she has her
prayer time during the day.

Let me finish with some of the more practical things that have
helped me. I use a prayer note book with the days of the month
marked at the top of the page. The first few pages are blank. In
these I have written those people and situations for which I pray
every day. As the prayer is answered I cross it out. Over the rest
of the month I spread the names of people and situations I am
committed to pray for. This method has helped me tremendously
to disipline my thoughts. A prayer partner is invaluable. I tell
women that their husband should be a real prayer partner. I see
the need, however, for a man or woman to have a prayer partner
of the same sex. To meet with this person regularly or to be able
to pray with him or her on the phone has been a really enriching
experience for me.

I also have over my kitchen sink several little ornaments. These
represent different friends and as I wash up I enjoy thinking and
praying for the individuals represented there.

The prayers of Paul are also used by me frequently. They are
so big – and I realise over and over again the value of asking big.
If you ask big you get big. If you ask small you get small.

As I finish, my heart is overwhelmed with wonder, not at the
way my prayer life is and has been, but that all my sin and guilt
have been coped with through the blood of Christ, so that I have
free access to the Father. I marvel that he actually loves me and
keeps on loving me. Finally, I wonder too as I remember that
heaven is ahead and prayer will be a face to face experience with
him who loved me and gave himself for me.

8 Sue Sinclair:
Butterfly Prayer-life

I love to watch the peacock butterflies on the buddleias in our garden. Butterflies thrive in the sunshine. Sometimes they pause for a moment in their constant movement and open their bright wings to the sun. Then they're off, darting away again. At other times they like to rest, still, for quite a period, absorbing the warmth and light from the sun.

My life of prayer as a busy house-wife is rather like that of the peacock butterfly. I am generally conscious of my heavenly Father's surrounding presence and love, as I tackle all the things that have to be done in the day – things that often need doing two at a time! I stir the custard and listen to somebody's spellings. I visualise the contents of the fridge and scratch together a lunch of left-overs while I plait two yellow pigtails. I'm here, there and everywhere, just like the butterfly. But the moments do come when I pause, open my wings to the sun and talk to my Father God. Sometimes it's only a brief word, sometimes for a longer period of time. This is what brings life into perspective for me.

I cannot remember a time when I didn't believe in God. It is a special privilege to be brought up as I was, in a family where, talking to your heavenly Father, was a normal part of life, just as normal as chatting to Mum by the kitchen stove.

My parents demonstrated a pattern which I have been able to work out in my own family life. Max and I prayed for each of our children before they were born. When they were little babies we used to pray out loud over them. I remember Naomi, our first child, in a battered old blue cot in Africa. We leaned over the sides and prayed each night out loud. There was a picture of two rabbits on the wall and underneath the words, *'The Lord is good to all'* taken from Psalm 145. Every night when we had finished praying we would point to the picture and repeat the verse. Naomi listened while we prayed and then pointed her own chubby hand at the picture on the wall. Who knows how much she was really taking in, even though she couldn't talk!

Later, as the children grew, I found prayer to be a wonderful help. 'Mummy, why did Pegleg have to die?' Anna's sad, round face peered into mine. It had been very bleak to discover our pet lamb's body, stiff and cold in the corner of his paddock that morning. But, what a relief to be able to say, 'I don't know Annie, but I do know that God knows all about it and he loves us very much. There are lots of sad things that happen in this world, that we just don't understand, but he does. We must keep on trusting him. Let's pray about it.' I am sure God wants us to tell him how we feel: *'Cast all your anxieties on him because he cares for you,'* the Bible tells us (1 Peter 5.7).

Habits, like cleaning your teeth, are learnt as much by example as by instruction. After breakfast there's a mass exodus in our house to the basin for a good scrub round the mouth. Children pick up the habit of prayer and make it their own by the example of adults. Max and I read the Bible and pray every morning before we get up. It's a way of keeping in touch with the Lord and building your relationship with him. The children have begun to read and pray, on their own each morning, using Scripture Union Bible reading notes appropriate to their ages, to help them. In the evenings, the children change into their night clothes and then scurrry back downstairs for family prayers. The best times are when Dad's at home and we spread ourselves on the floor round the sittingroom fire. We collect up all the things to pray about and then share them out so that everyone has a chance to pray. Ben invariably insists on praying for Daddy regardless of what he's doing.

As a child I was used to saying Grace before meals. It seemed to me positively vulgar not to pause and thank the Lord before plunging into one of my Mum's delicious stews. Saying Grace is a way of acknowledging that everything I have comes ultimately from him.

Max and I have made Grace a habit in our family. Sometimes we all join hands and sing it. Alas though, one Sunday, the inevitable happened. Max and I were invited out to tea with Naomi aged four and Anna three, by a rather posh lady. The long table clad in starched white, positively creaked under the weight of cakes and chocolate biscuits, quivering red jellies and soft white sandwiches with their crusts removed. We sat and stared. 'Do start, won't you, she nodded and bent to pour China tea from a fluted teapot covered in roses. An awkward silence, shifty looks sideways, then a clear insistent child's voice, 'But we *can't* start; we haven't said Grace.' Oh, the embarrassment of our hostess! Max grasped hold of the situation and thanked the Lord as simply and naturally as he could. Then the whole affair was underway.

The family constantly tease me because, when it's my turn to give thanks, I completely forget about the food and have quite a chat with the Lord over whatever is on my mind. Then I remember and hurriedly tack the food on the end of the prayer.

Our aim as parents is to make the idea of talking to the Lord a spontaneous part of everyday life. 'Let's pray about it,' becomes a natural response to any joy, dilemma, sadness or frustration. It doesn't have to be on bended knee in a quiet place alone. I can pray as I hang out the washing, iron the shirts or stand in a supermarket queue. What an amazing idea – an invisible telephone line to the Boss of the universe and it's never engaged and it's never ignored.

Prayer is the most mysterious thing. How is it that almighty God should choose to involve me, mixed up, selfish, fickle human being that I am, in his eternal plans and purposes? I can't understand it, but I *do* know that he has told us to pray, that prayer changes people and situations and that he wants me simply to trust him, whatever the answer may be.

Six years ago I discovered in a very direct way, just how significant prayer is. Max and I were driving to Devon with baby Ben asleep on the back seat of the car. Driving provides a great opportunity to pray – provided you remember *not* to close your eyes! We felt as though we had reached a kind of plateau in our lives and asked God to show us the way forward. The answer came soon enough at six o'clock the next morning, as we began our return journey to Kent. There was an orange Capri coming towards us on the road. Without warning, it began to cross the centre line and then, suddenly, terrifyingly, it came straight at us. In the devastating impact, Max's neck was broken and in one split second his life was changed. He was paralysed from the shoulders down, in effect, a head without a body. Somehow Benjie and I remained unhurt.

In the hard times that followed, I learnt more of the wonderful meaning of prayer. Max was taken to Stoke Mandeville. I stayed until he had passed the critical period. Just imagine my thrill and wonder when, after being told my husband would, very probably, be paralysed for the rest of his life and be confined to a wheelchair, his limbs began to tingle and gradually, painfully, some feeling and movement began to return. Then, after six months had passed, he actually walked out of the hospital ward and came home.

I don't know why God chose to let Max recover, but I believe there is a purpose behind everything he does, even though we cannot see it or only catch the odd glimpse. I believe this was the Lord's answer to the prayers of hundreds of Christians who felt prompted to pray, and I thank him from my heart. When, within hours of the car crash I heard that people from all over the country were praying for Max, I *knew* what being part of the body of Christ, was all about. As the Bible puts it, '*If one part suffers, every part suffers with it; if one part is honoured; every part rejoices with it. Now you are the body of Christ and each one of you is a part of it*' (I Co. 12,26,27)

I knew too, in my bones, that God *was* beginning to answer our prayer on the car drive to Devon (what an age ago that seemed now). I felt as though a stone had been dropped, with the Lord's permission, into the pool of life and the ripples would begin to radiate outwards.

Though this was a time of great testing for me, I seemed to be buoyed up like a hovercraft on a cushion of other people's prayers. I felt like the paralysed man in the gospels, carried to Jesus by four real friends, who believed and cared enough to demolish a roof in order to place him right at Jesus's feet. '*When Jesus saw their faith*,' he acted. The Bible seemed to come alive to me and I wanted to tell others about my Lord, while my husband lay staring at the ceiling, his limbs like lead. Then many opportunitiies presented themselves.

The praying that I did at that time was not so much that Max would get better. I had the sense that God would do what he thought best. But my praying was a sort of verbalising of the thoughts churning round in my head. There were long hours between hospital visits, there was chubby faced one year-old Ben, there was me with my churning thoughts and there was an old borrowed push chair. So off we marched. I got to know the lanes and paths around the hospital like the back of my hand. Most of the time I was verbalising my thoughts.

With the background knowledge I had from the Bible, I began to see that suffering of all kinds is only normal in a world that is blighted by evil. I also saw that God has the ability to make wonderful things emerge from suffering. I realised that the greatest example of this is the way God used Satan's most terrible attack on Jesus, when he, the sinless Son of God, was nailed to a rough wooden gallows by evil men and left there to die. God turned the tables on Satan and used this most horrible crucifixion to be the way that we can find complete forgiveness, and experience a new life. Because Jesus came alive again, defeating death, we can experience his life within us, as our constant friend.

I remember pushing Ben in the old pushchair up a hill by a rugged stone wall. The boulders were hard and rough, like the situation Max was in. But here and there, between the boulders the fragile purple flowers and the patterned leaves of Toad flax hung; beauty blossoming from something cold and harsh to feel.

I prayed then that the Lord would bring something good from the trial we were experiencing. And now, six years have passed and I am overwhelmed by the way God has honoured that prayer, in ways I had never thought of. Blessing has flowed out of Max's suffering, like a river, touching many lives, mine included.

Now, here I am living my busy butterfly life. I still find it easiest to pray when I walk alone. Natural beauty and especially that of the sky, causes me to praise him as Creator. The rhythm of my walking keeps my brain active. When I sit or kneel alone in a quiet room, pall begins to descend and my thoughts can easily wander off into nothingness.

Every day there are school runs to make in the car. At first they seemed very tedious. Then I realised what excellent, tailor-made opportunities they were for butterfly prayers. I bring each child before the Lord and surround them with prayer as they go to face the challenges, demands and temptations of another day at school.

There's a noisy, irritating little ogre sitting in the corner of our kitchen. He's waiting to get at me, just as I switch on the mixer to make a jelly cream or sit down to tea with the family. On many days I'm tempted to regard the telephone that way. It rings a great deal. However, I've tried praying as I advance to put an end to his noise and, as I pray, I discover there's actually a person on the end of the line. Then the irritation just disappears in a puff of smoke.

Our home is in a village. I keep Thursday mornings free and walk up the muddy track to a friend's house. There, a handful of us housewives sit round a coal fire in a small, snug room. We read the Bible together and then we pray. The house is perched on the hillside and from the windows, the ground slopes away, down to the other houses amongst the trees. In our prayers we bring to the Lord each family by name in the different areas. We pray over what we have read together and how it can become part of our lives; we also share our own joys, sorrows and problems. Praying together is a very strengthening experience.

It will add strength too, in a marriage, to pray together. The Bible says '*Do not let the sun go down while you are still angry, and do not give the devil a foothold.*' How could we pray together at the close of the day with anger, bitterness or jealously seething inside us? Keeping short accounts by praying together can keep a marriage in one piece.

In the mornings Max and I get out a well thumbed blue file labelled 'prayer list'. There are some people we want to pray for regularly, so we've entered them on pages marked Days 1 to 7. We ourselves may never know the results of these prayers, but I see it this way. Each time we pray it's like paying a deposit into the prayer-bank of that person. When he sees fit, the Lord will withdraw from their account, the blessing and help that they need.

I've also discovered that prayer means action. Sometimes I am shown how I myself can become part of the answer to my own prayer. There are other times when I pray not really knowing what I should pray for. How good it is then to come across a verse like, '*We do not know what we ought to pray, but the Spirit himself intercedes for us with groans that words cannot express.*' (Romans 8.26)!

There are answers, I suspect, which *have* come, but I've never even noticed – probably because I was too busy looking the wrong way! I've found it a help to keep a notebook and record the answers to prayer that I can identify. Claiming things the Lord has done in the past can deal a hefty blow to the doubts that Satan loves to plant in our hearts.

What extraordinary freedom we have in prayer. My thoughts can shoot out five thousand miles to the simple mudwalled home of our missionary friends in Uganda and become involved in the work they are doing. I can reach out and touch the life of that tense, fidgeting lady in the surgery waiting room. I can pray at any time, anywhere. I am never alone.

When I was a teenager and part of a youth group, we would

carol sing round the old people's homes at Christmas. There was somewhere else we went, somewhere very special. Special, not because of the place, a dim room in a gaunt grey Victorian house, but because of the person there. She was a frail old lady. She couldn't see, she couldn't walk and she could only just hear, with a powerful hearing aid, but she radiated her love for the Lord Jesus. Her physical life was cramped, dark and shut in, but in her spirit, she was a free as a lark in a summer sky. Prayer was her main occupation, praying steadily for hundreds of missionary families in every corner of the world, using tapes that were sent to her. A seasoned traveller indeed!

Sometimes, as I go downstairs after saying goodnight to the children a voice sings out in the darkness, 'I love you.' How good it is to hear it said, even though I know it already. Perhaps that is partly why God invented prayer. He, our heavenly Father, just loves to hear his children call out to him in the darkness, 'I love you.'

9 Margaret Dehqani-Tafti: Living in the Presence of God

The bedroom door swung open with the smallest of creaks but that slight sound was enough to jerk me from the depths of peaceful sleep into fearfilled wakefulness. We were living in Iran, in that autumn of 1979, amidst the terrors and uncertainties of the Islamic Revolution, my husband being the first Persian Bishop of the tiny convert Anglican Church. The times were dangerous, and at that moment I knew with absolute certainty that the two men who slipped quietly into our bedroom in the early morning hours had come to kill.

Before I had time to think, one of them walked up to the bed, took aim and fired five shots, with his revolver held within two feet of my husband's head. The bullets thudded into the pillow within inches of where he lay, except for the one that went through my left hand as I reached out to grab the gun. Miraculously my husband was unhurt, and in that split second I was aware of what I can only describe as a blanket of prayer, so real that it was a physical, tangible thing, surrounding us both. At that critical moment, people whom we know (and many whom we do not know) were prompted to pray for us and our lives were spared.

Since that time we have been made far more aware of what we already knew – that our life, which was not taken away by those bullets, belongs to God and we hold it as a gift from him. And just as our life was preserved by prayer that night, it has to be sustained through prayer; for prayer simply means *living all of life in the presence of God*.

Of course, that is easy to say and difficult to do, for prayer is as complicated as life itself and with as many aspects. But basically it is a living relationship with God himself, which matures and grows over the years. We all know how long it takes to develop a deep and loving human relationship – living, talking, laughing, crying and fighting together; loving one another, forgiving and giving in to each other. And so it is with prayer. St Paul says, '*Pray without ceasing*.' This is only possible if it becomes a natural part of us like breathing. But on the other hand, the life of prayer also has to be learnt and struggled with, put into practice, failed in, and started again. How can these two aspects of prayer be merged together – relaxation and naturalness with struggle and learning? It is easy to become disappointed, or depressed, and to feel that prayer just isn't worth the effort. But as with anything worth while it needs perseverance and persistence, a willingness to fall down and to get up again; time for study and reading; worshipping with others, and practising the presence of God.

As women and mothers who have been aware of children growing up around us, or watched our own children grow up, we know so well how in the early years of life so much evolves round 'self'. But the healthy normal child who has seen love, discipline and training at home, slowly begins to mature, learning new attitudes, thinking about others, and building proper relationships. I often compare this with our position in God's presence. We start off as children – so selfish or shallow, so preoccupied with ourselves, always asking for things, please give, give, give. They may be very good things we are asking for – patience, love, forgiveness, and we must not despise these prayers, because any touch with God is of great value and God loves to give. But what would we feel like if our children only came to us to ask for more things? What a joy it is when we can just enjoy the company of those we love – when no words are needed because we sense their love and know that they are happy to be with us. I believe God must be so happy when we can just sit and think about him, enjoying his company and loving him like that. This, too, is prayer.

Where I lived in Iran it got very cold in the winter and yet in a sheltered corner the sun's rays could be amazingly warm. I remember often feeling physically cold and yet, when I retreated for a minute to a sunny sheltered place, the warmth quickly penetrated my whole being, melting the chilliness within me. In life we also experience cold spells – times when we think God has abandoned us to face illness, suffering, unemployment, or whatever it may be, alone. That is the time when we specially need to spend time with God: to pray and give his warmth and joy a chance to flood through us. Of course that is not easy. When my heart is cold I find it difficult to pray. It needs discipline. But if I try to pray, then perhaps it will mean more to God than when it comes easily for me. And this sort of prayer does not have to be words – simply an unspoken reaching out for God, a longing to know him better, and a willingness to let him have control of the situation. Some lovely words have been found written on the walls of a cellar in Germany after World War II:

> *'I believe in the sun, even when it is not shining,*
> *I believe in love even when I feel it not,*
> *I believe in God even when he is silent.'*

I was born and brought up in a missionary home in the country of Iran where my father was first the Headmaster of a boys' college, and then became Bishop of our Church there. I later married a young Persian man who was ordained and in charge of one of the churches. We were blessed with four children – three girls and one boy, and before the fourth child was born my husband had been consecrated as the new Bishop, when my father retired.

For years when the children were growing up, life seemed so busy and tiring. All my energy and time seemed to go into keeping the home and seeing to the physical needs of the family and the visitors who flowed through our home. Often at night there was no thought but to go to bed and get some sleep before the business of tomorrow was upon me. And, of course, I am not the only one to face this problem. So many women round the world are on this wearisome treadmill of constant activity which seems to give us no time to deepen our spiritual life. But I discovered that we don't have to find more time (which is impossible) to pray, but we do have to turn the busy life and all it contains into prayer. I don't believe we shall be judged by the amount of time we spend on our knees (though this is part of life). What really matters is our *longing* for a closer walk with God, and we can develop this aim in the busiest life. While the family are young we may go for months (possibly years) without being able to have a regular set time for our personal quiet prayer, but what matters is that we still continue to *want* to make it part of life, and when it does become possible again, to fit it into our day. This is unlikely to happen unless we make it a habit to turn every job that comes our way – be it cleaning, shopping, cooking, sitting up at night with a crying child, washing the dishes, helping our children with their homework, or anything else, into a prayer.

What are called 'arrow prayers' can become a habit which will transform our lives because they continually turn our attention to God. If ever busy housewives had to choose a patron saint, surely it would be Brother Lawrence. He lived in the seventeenth century and after being a soldier and later a hermit, he entered a Carmelite Monastery where he was given charge of the kitchen. We know what a busy life working in a kitchen can be, but Brother Lawrence tried to put into practice the continual sense of God's presence in all his humble work, and this was prayer to him. The famous prayer called '*The Kitchen Prayer*' or '*Lord of the Pots and Pans*' could be his prayer:

'*Lord of pots and pans and things,*
   Since I've not got time to be
A saint by doing lovely things
   or watching late with You
Or dreaming in the dawn light
   or storming heaven's gates,
Make me a saint by getting meals
   and washing up the plates.

Although I must have Martha hands
   I have a Mary mind
And when I black the boots and shoes
   Your sandals, Lord, I find.
I think of how they trod the earth
   What time I scrub the floor
Accept this meditation, Lord,
   I haven't time for more.'.

To quote Bishop Stephen Neill '*The Christian, developing the habit of turning a hundred times a day to consider in every situation what the will of God may be, finds that his life too is growing into the pattern of an unbroken dialogue with God.*'

Does this sound too simple? It is certainly *not* easy and needs working towards – perseverance is involved. I have watched our children trying hard to learn a musical instrument and slowly over the years becoming better and better – enjoying it more themselves and giving more pleasure to others. Prayer is just the same.

86

You have to struggle with it. I have often felt like giving up altogether because I have failed over and over again. There have been times when I have experienced deep peace, and at other times I have just had to trust that God understands, and hang on to the flicker of faith that still existed.

'Waiting on God' suggests that we go to God and find out from him what he wants us to do in every situation. Often we have to learn to 'wait' for an answer, and this doesn't come easily for most of us who want to know what the next move is going to be quickly and make plans and decisions.

One of the pitfalls is that too often I have tried to separate life and prayer. I thought that I could make my own plans and then ask God to bless them. But that just doesn't work. Life and prayer must go hand in hand – like a child putting his hand into the hand of his mother or father and walking into a foggy night with confidence. I have had a copy of some famous words hanging in our hall all our married life:

> *I said to the man who stood at the gate of the year, 'Give me a light that I may tread safely into the unknown.' And he replied, 'Go out into the darkness and put your hand into the hand of God. That shall be better to you than light and safer than a known way.'*

I believe that the many times I have read them (consciously and unconsciously) have had a far deeper effect than I can ever realise. They remind me that we can't always choose and plan our lives; there will be times when we just have to go out into the dark and unknown. This can bring with it fears, conflicting emotions and worries unless we learn to develop this child-father relationship, and having put our hand into the hand of God, trust that he is in full control and that even if we are surrounded by fog, the ground beneath us is solid.

Our church community in Iran was a very small one. We were very conscious of living in a non-Christian society, and we had to realise that our children were going to face particular problems as they grew up and would really have to work out their own faith in the face of different ideas around them.

For many years I prayed that God would use our family in the building up of his tiny church in Iran. Did I know what I was asking, or what it might cost? Certainly not, and yet I believe I was sincere in my praying. What has happened has indeed been costly and very different from anything I could imagine. When I prayed I certainly didn't imagine God would build up his church by shattering our family. When we try to do what God wants us to do we think all will be well with us. I had tried to 'wait on God' (Psalm 25.5) and to want God to use us – but I expected good results. How easy it is to bargain with God in our prayers and say we will try to do God's will, but of course expect something in return.

When the Revolution hit Iran it was quite obvious that the Muslim fanatics would choose our church and family as one of their targets. Over a period of some months our home was raided – demands were made on my husband which he could not accept. I watched him being arrested and taken off by armed guards – later to be freed. Pressures of one kind and another continued, and then the attempt to kill my husband was made. Somehow the type of prayers asking for safety or for relief of problems became meaningless. God has never guaranteed freedom from physical danger but he has promised his grace and strength through prayer life with him. The only meaningful prayer was – '*Lord, deepen my faith and my trust in you*' In the darkness and uncertainty that surrounded us, I needed to know my hand in God's hand in such a way that faith was deepened and trust strengthened. I believe God suffers when he watches the result of giving his children freedom in this world – the way they hurt each other. He weeps in the fact of the world's tragedies. But it would hurt him even more if we failed to use the grace and strength and peace which he puts at our disposal through prayer. He has promised, but we have to accept these gifts. Evil never becomes good in disguise, yet God can transform it if we allow him to do so. There are mysteries and we cannot expect to understand. But I do know that if I had allowed resentment and hate to develop in my mind and thoughts, my prayer life would certainly have been damaged and the flow of God's spirit into my life and those particular circumstances would have been blocked.

After the attack on my husband's life when he was miracuously kept alive, our family was separated by distance because my husband had to attend church meetings in the Middle East, and having left Iran, was advised by the church to delay his return, although he had had every intention of returning in spite of the circumstances. It is difficult to describe the confusion of mind and emotions which occurs when we have to face the unknown . . . if we are made redundant . . . if we have a bad accident . . . if a loved one dies . . . We just don't know how to face the future. It can make us mentally ill. The only solution is to turn to God and somehow hand over the distress to him. It must be a *conscious* decision. We must realise that *there is no other way*.

I experienced this unbearable physical and mental pain when, six months after my husband had left the country, our only son, just twenty-four years old, was murdered by the fanatics who had tried to kill his father. Life seemed finished and prayer impossible. Only the word '*Why?*' But in the commotion of emotions the thought instilled on my heart was, '*Be still and know that I am God*'. Unless our thoughts are quietened we cannot be aware of God's presence, and this quietness is a gift from God, which we must accept in the silence of prayer. Words no longer matter. We just have to KNOW that God is with us in the midst of our distress.

I believe we have to cultivate this calmness and quietness throughout life. Silent prayer has to be practised over and over again in the happiest days, to be a possibility in times of trouble. When we are really happy, do we sit down and thank God and try and just keep that quiet in his presence? Unless we acknowledge him and his presence in our 'good days' how can we immediately make contact on our 'bad days'? Again, my children help me to understand this more clearly. Suppose the only time they turned to me was when they needed something or were faced with a problem, and never told me of their joys and pleasures or let me share in their happy times or showed that they enjoyed being in my company. I know how sad and incomplete I would feel. Also, I probably wouldn't be able to help them in their need anyhow because our relationship would not be right. May our prayer be that God will help us to use all the circumstances of our life to produce in us fruits of holiness rather than fruits of sin:

> to use disappointments to have more patience;
> to use danger to have more courage;
> to use the unknown to have more perseverance;
> to use pain to have more endurance;
> to use wrongs done to us to have more forgiveness;
> to use joy and happiness to be more thankful;
> to use pain and loss to endure more faithfully;
> to use every circumstance to have more love.

Life is made up of these different circumstances. All of us have to experience some or most of them. By going through them prayerfully we are better equipped to understand others facing such situations, and what we have learnt can be put into prayer for them, making us much more sensitive people.

Another aspect of prayer life which I believe is essential is gratitude. Unless we can develop and cultivate a spirit of gratitude and thanksgiving our life is dark and dead. It is through praise that we realise a sense of God's majesty and glory and greatness and lovingkindness. Sometimes I am ashamed to compare the proportion of 'thanksgiving' to 'asking' in my prayers – but if we only open our eyes we realise how many blessings we can count (and we certainly don't deserve any of them) and the thanks we give are a prayer of worship.

By being grateful we mature – we learn to look away from ourselves to the source of all life and all that we have. Everything we have is from God but how often do we acknowledge this? To say 'Thank you' gives us a new perspective and enriches our lives. To say 'Thank you' is to pray.

We all need help and guidance of some sort or another and of course each individual may find different things helpful. I have found that to have a private book of prayers to which I can add new prayers and quotes has been a great help to me. Thirty-four years ago I bought a small book called *A Diary of Private Prayer* by John Baillie (published by Oxford University Press), which provides prayers which are intended to help us in our morning and evening devotions for each day of a month. For each day there is also a blank page on which you can add your own prayers or intercessions as you choose. When I see that this book is still available in bookshops it makes me realise it has been a very popular one. One of the few things I brought out of Iran with me when we had to leave in a hurry was this book of prayers, as over the years it has become more and more meaningful to me. So often I have been aware of how I have misused those prayers, or mishandled the treasure of thoughts included in them, or just failed to use them, but somehow the desire and longing has returned and I have been able to turn back to them. At intervals during those years I added quotations and prayers which I came across and wanted to keep. One such quotation is, '*Prayer doesn't necessarily change things for you, but it changes you for things.*' If our desire for God is allowed to grow, it certainly doesn't mean we shall always be given what *we want*, but it will change us to be ready to accept our lot in life and even more want *God's will* to be done.

I remember so clearly as a child kneeling beside my father at a service in church. I respected him greatly and indeed loved him very much, and thought he could never do anything wrong. Also in my childish way I thought that to pray you must have your eyes shut, and if you opened them you failed terribly. But that day I risked opening my eyes to see whether my father's eyes were shut. To my initial horror I saw they were open, but then I realised that he was gazing at the cross on the altar. I shall never forget the lesson that has gradually over the years dawned on me, that prayer is far more than having my eyes shut tight and asking God for things. Prayer is gazing on God and understanding life through his eyes, and realising that prayer and life must be closely inter-mingled and faced with our eyes open.

> *'Breathe on me, Breath of God,*
> *Fill me with life anew;*
> *That I may love what Thou dost love*
> *And do what Thou wouldst do.*
>
> *Breathe on me, Breath of God,*
> *Until my heart is pure;*
> *Until with Thee I will one will*
> *To do and to endure.'*

10 Marion Ashton:
Prayer's Upward Path

It was a beautiful sunny Saturday in May. The Bristol Girl Crusaders, of whom I was one, were enjoying their Birthday Party in the garden of what was then Carfax Missionary Training College. After tea and games, we went into the Hall for a short and informal meeting at which Miss Ivy Naish, one of the students, was to speak to us. Her talk only lasted a few minutes and was based on the words, *'Barabbas or Jesus which is called Christ?'* and presented us with a choice to be made between serving Satan or serving the Lord Jesus. This thought pierced me like a sword. I couldn't say I was definitely a Christian but I did *not* want to go through life serving Satan; of that I was quite clear.

All that weekend, a battle went on inside me until I got down on my knees by my bed and said something like this: Lord Jesus, I believe you died for me. I want to know for sure that my sins are forgiven; I want to know for sure that I am a real Christian; I want to know for sure that I am a child of God. You promised that *'him that comes to me I will in no wise cast out'*; I'm coming to you and am going to hold to it that you've heard this prayer and will not cast me out. I had prayed before, but this was the first desperate prayer, which I had every intention *must* be answered. And it was! It was not many days after that there came into my heart the quiet, deep certainty that he had received me, that I could say, I'm a child of God; I'm a true Christian. In this way, my path of prayer started.

I have one outstanding memory belonging to those early days of learning to pray and that is of the first time I opened my mouth to pray in front of others. We had decided to have a little prayer meeting before the Crusader class on Sundays, and on the day that we were to have the first one I knew that I must pray. I was *very* nervous and all the way there I went over the words I intended to say. There were just a few of us girls there, and, I think, two of our leaders, both students at the College and probably not many years older than we were, but thought by us to be very adult and very experienced in all Christian matters! Then came the moment when, somehow, I got my mouth open and said my prayer. My voice did not seem to come out of me, it sounded as if it came from somewhere else detached from myself! But the ice was broken, and I am glad it was broken early. I still don't always find it easy to pray in a large prayer meeting, but to pray out loud in small groups of like-minded people or with some close friend has been one of the greatest joys of the Pathway. I am so grateful that I have always had friends with whom I can pray.

It is over fifty years now since that first desperate prayer and I find it difficult to say what have been the most important lessons learnt. I find two particular difficulties: First, that there is so much to say and so many different aspects to prayer; then, on the other hand, there is so much that cannot be shared because it has taken place behind the 'closed door' of which the Lord Jesus spoke in Matthew 6.6. I also sympathise with a ninety year-old Christian friend of ours, who wrote in his last letter to us before he died, that one morning he had said to himself, '*John, I don't think you know much about prayer*'! I suppose it is the same with any worthwhile subject that the more we know, the more we realise that there are great areas that we don't know or about which we only know a very little. That surely must be so of prayer, if it is a vitally important part of our relationship with the living, almighty God.

That's where I want to start because, to me, it is the most important thing about prayer. Prayer is the most vital part of my living relationship with one who is my Saviour, Lord, Friend, and Father – the only one who knows and understands me perfectly, and who can enter the hidden depths of my being. Quite apart from special times set apart for prayer, I agree with the hymn writer who says:

'*Prayer is the Christian's vital breath,
The Christian's native air.*'

Dr Campbell Morgan, writing about the words of the Lord Jesus in Luke 18:1 'Men should always pray' says 'not words necessarily, not words at all; but an attitude of life.' Dr Alexander Whyte, in his book 'Lord Teach Us To Pray' describes this attitude as that of David expressed in Psalm 16:8 'I have set the Lord always before me'. I do believe that my path has become increasingly like that, over the years, in spite of all the mistakes, failures and inadequacies that I see in many aspects of my prayer life. Prayer – the native air of my relationship with the Lord; prayer – that which I desire to be the constant attitude of my life. In this living, on-going relationship I make endless requests for strength, for guidance, for help, for everything I need: and He endlessly gives, often in the simplest of ways. Or, I may not ask anything, but just talk to him.

I have also always found it necessary to have regular time set apart for prayer and, for years, had many struggles over finding that time and keeping to it. The years of being a medical student and then the years in Kenya when our home was full of children and often visitors as well, were ones in which it was not always easy to keep a regular daily time for prayer. Nor was it easy then, for my husband and I to maintain a regular daily time for prayer together, a habit which we always felt was essential in our marriage. As the years have gone by, it has become much easier and now I know that, for me, nothing substitutes for the early morning time set apart for the Lord. I, personally, find the morning to be far the best time. At night, try as I may, I can do very little serious praying without falling asleep! The only exceptions to that are the occasional times when the need for prayer so grips me that I can't go to sleep!

One valuable lesson I learnt over the years of struggling was that God's blessing did not *depend* on my having that special time of prayer. I used to think it did and would feel guilty and not expect his blessing if I missed it. I discovered that his blessing depended on his grace, not on any kind of achievement on my part. What mattered was my *relationship* with him; and he knew that I wanted the time and intended to struggle on towards regularity. I have written down a quotation from Neville Ward's book *The Use of Praying*. He says, '*It's impossible to explore the world of prayer with interest and hope of discovery if you feel guilty because you do not pray or when you do not pray. The subject never comes alive to guilt but it does to curiosity and interest.*'

Not only did I have struggles over establishing a regular time for prayer, but I have had many struggles about the plan to be followed within the time. In what order should I proceed? Should it always be praise first? Or, maybe it ought to be confession first?

Should it be the Bible first? Or prayer first, then the Bible? Should I make lists of people and situations to be prayed for every day? Once a week? Once a month? Or should I just let the Holy Spirit lead? Whenever I heard someone speak about his or her own pattern, I would think that that was very good and would try to copy it! But I always found that to copy someone else or to make my own rigid framework led to bondage and stifled the life and moving of the Spirit. So, I would smash the framework and start again! My pattern now is reasonably orderly, and I do use lists of people and special needs, but they have become reminders and servants rather than tyrannical masters. I need flexibility if there is to be life. As I get older, I increasingly know that the time needs to be a leisurely one. I need time just to relax before the Lord.

One joyous discovery I made was from the Psalms. I had heard so often that we should start with praise and had tried so hard to do that. At times it was not difficult, but at other times every effort would be swamped by what I was feeling over some problem, or just what I was *feeling*! Then, as I read the Psalms, I realised that sometimes the Psalmist starts with praises and sometimes he starts with his distress and ends with praise. Psalm 69 is a good example: He starts with waters up to his neck, sinking and weary with crying. He ends with a glorious song of praise. This has helped me to relax and to give myself up to the problem, or the exercise of heart and mind and talk to the Lord about it. Over and over again on these occasions, there comes the time when the problem is not necessarily solved but quietness and comfort creep into my heart and I know the Lord has entered in. *That* is an experience which very quickly turns to praise.

I do try to pray for quite a large number of people and, at one time, when I was feeling the total inadequacy of these prayers, I remembered that at least once Paul said, '*I mention you in my prayers*', and was encouraged. About the same time, I found myself thinking of John's account of the Feeding of the Five Thousand in John 6. The Lord Jesus said, '*Gather up the fragments left over, that nothing may be lost*'. I do believe that the Lord who took such care that no fragment of food should be lost also gathers up all our fragments of prayer and one day, when we get to heaven, we shall marvel to know that none of those little fragments of prayer were lost. I don't only have to wait for heaven to get some confirmation of this. There have been many times (which I refuse to think of as coincidence) when, in making mention of someone, I have said to the Lord, 'Lord, I would love to know how that one is getting on'; and within a week, sometimes within twenty-four hours, I've received a letter telling me what I have wanted to know. I know there is a mystery about what is called 'unanswered prayer', or about delayed answers, and I know something of the agony connected with this; but one of the greatest wonders to me is the frequency with which God *does* answer what seem to me just fragments. In connection with what are called unanswered prayers, my deep conviction is that God always *responds* to the prayers of his children and where there seems to be long delay, it is never delay in his working, but only in our seeing what he is doing. I'm glad that answers are limited by his will, for his will is that of infinite love and infinite wisdom. I am increasingly aware that I don't know how to pray and need the Holy Spirit's leading in praying for myself, for others and for all kinds of situations. One of the things the Holy Spirit has often to handle first is my own personal feelings. I had an example of this when the Falklands Crisis was at its height, before active fighting had started. I woke in the middle of the night gripped with a gnawing anxiety. If fighting started, where would it end? Would it spread, as some said, and be the beginning of a Third World War? I cried to the Lord to prevent the beginning of fighting. After a short time, I realised that my main desire was to get rid of my anxiety! If only I could be sure there would be a solution other than fighting, then I'd lose this awful anxiety! This realisation resulted in my changing my prayer and beginning to pray that the Lord would take away my anxiety and enable me to trust him quietly, whatever might happen. I reminded myself of his absolute sovereignty and that '*he is our refuge and strength though the earth be removed*', as we read in Psalm 46. Gradually, my anxiety died away and stayed away. After that, I was able to ask the Lord to guide me as to how to pray for the whole situation. I often find this principle important when praying for someone's healing, or for the needs of those who are nearest to me. How I need to be free to be directed by the Holy Spirit in my praying, and not just by my own anxiety or pain!

The Bible is inextricably joined to my path of prayer and is a vital part of my relationship with the Lord. I spend part of the morning times of quiet with him, reading the Bible. I go systematically through the whole, but not straight through from Genesis to Revelation. I usually take an Old Testament book and a New Testament one alternately. Sometimes I use a devotional Commentary, sometimes I don't; sometimes I read through a book quite rapidly, sometimes much more slowly. Prayer must include God speaking to me as well as my speaking to him; and the Bible is his chief way of speaking to me. I hardly ever find that some particular verse leaps out of the page to me! I just know that as I read and meditate and pray over it, God is speaking to me. I may experience that as his *doing* something in me. For instance, his taking away of anxiety is his way of saying to me, '*Don't be afraid*'.

I try to turn what I read into praise and prayer for myself and others. What a rich book the Bible is on the subject of prayer! The whole prayer book of Psalms, full of expressions of prayer and praise; so many recorded prayers of so many different kinds of people. I need to go so much further in making these mine. There are Paul's prayers in the New Testament; and in the Old Testament, one that I particularly love is Nehemiah's in Nehemiah 9. To read that prayer, which is an account of God's repeated acts of compassion in spite of all his people's unfaithfulness is a sure way of causing my heart to glow at the steadfast love of the Lord.

But, best of all is the window we have into the prayer life of the Lord Jesus himself. I love to think about this. I was encouraged when I realised that it's impossible, from his life, to support any particular pattern for times of prayer; but from beginning to end of his public ministry there are references to his praying. *He* found it necessary to get away repeatedly into solitary places to pray. *He* taught much about prayer and gave us the pattern of prayer. Above all, *he* introduced us to the Father. As I think of him in prayer, I find myself praying again in the final words of a hymn which I've already quoted:

The path of prayer Thyself hast trod;
Lord, teach ME how to pray.

Over and over again, I have experienced God's faithfulness in answering prayer when preparing to speak at a meeting and when the moment for speaking has come. Numerous times I have cried to the Lord in my emptiness and told him that I don't know what to say or how to handle a subject, and always he gradually gives the thoughts and makes clear the message. However weak and nervous I have felt beforehand (and I have very frequently felt that), when the moment has come he has taken away the nervousness and given strength.

I owe a great deal on my path of prayer to people who have prayed for me and for my family. My own path would have been far poorer without those prayers. There is one period of my life when I needed the love and strength of those prayers more than at any other time: it was when I couldn't pray for myself. During the long dark days of a serious depressive illness, I could not pray. Through that period which amounted to three years, others prayed for me. Some close to me and others who hardly knew me prayed believingly for my full recovery. Looking back, it feels as if they carried me through, and I am deeply grateful. I believe those prayers played a large part in my complete recovery and in the fact that I came through to a greater emotional freedom than I had known before and a wonderful experience of spiritual renewal.

Shortly after my recovery, the words from Ephesians 2.18, *We have access . . . to the Father* came alive to me in a special way, and have had a deep effect on my prayer life ever since. I had known that verse for years, but had often fallen into the trap of trying to put things right before coming to him, especially things connected with my feelings and reactions. The truth now dawned on me afresh that, through the Lord Jesus, I really do have free access to the Father, JUST AS I AM. And not just to come to him but to *live* in his presence – a child in the Father's house. The result has been greater openness, greater honesty and reality and, I think, greater childlikeness in doing what the Psalmist invites us to do in Psalm 62.8, *Pour out your heart before him*. Recently, I found the following quote in *The Christian Experience of Forgiveness* by H. R. Mackintosh: *The Father in mercy has taken us into his personal communion and let us see in Christ that we have unrestricted access to himself.*

'Unrestricted access' – What an amazing fact!

It is that which is the essence of my path of prayer.

11 Patricia St John:
Lessons I have Learnt about Prayer

Having been born of parents to whom prayer was as natural as breathing, my thoughts about praying go back a long way. I was probably taught to say my prayers as I learned to talk and although I remember noticing, at a very early age, that I did not exactly get everything I asked for overnight, there were enough almost miraculous answers to do with pet rabbits, broken toys and numerous lost articles to make me feel that there really was someone listening. Although I could not always persuade 'him' to do what I wanted, it was certainly worth trying.

It was probably somewhere between the ages of six and eight that I came to understand that I could enter into a lasting relationship with him and choose to become his child. My mother taught me Isaiah 43.1, and I remember kneeling down and telling God that my name was Patricia St John and, if he had really called me by my name, then here I was. I knew that my prayer was heard and that something had happened. From then on, prayer became more personal, like talking to someone like my father, who loved me very much.

The growing-up years flew by with the usual peaks and troughs. I was sometimes wildly enthusiastic; sometimes on the point of giving it all up. I prayed for my school friends, for the children I taught when I left school, and later on, as a member of a small, struggling hospital Christian union, we prayed for the conversion of our fellow nurses. Each era seemed all-absorbing and, as I passed from one phase of life into the next, I tended to lose the urgency in praying for some who had previously seemed so important. After all, in most cases nothing much had happened, so why go on? Their faces faded in the surge of new interests and, little by little, I ceased to pray for them.

It is only now that I am beginning to realise that, although *we* may forget, God does not forget sincere intercessory prayer. We may fail, but '*He remains faithful*'. Some of the answered prayers of the Bible illustrate this; Abraham and Sarah, Zacharias and Elizabeth, had long since ceased to pray for a child when the angel told them that their prayer had been heard. Daniel had prayed for many years at his open window, apparently in vain, before Gabriel said, '*At the beginning of your prayer the commandment came forth*'. Certainly no true prayer, prayed in the name of Jesus, has ever been lost or mislaid; but it may take a lifetime and many links in the chain of prayer and circumstances to order the events of history, or to bring someone to repentance and faith. It is humbling and thrilling to hear from people, sometimes long forgotten but once earnestly prayed for, who have, in later years, come to Christ in totally different circumstances. It has taught me that if, in the changes and pressures of life, some names have to be put aside, then I need to do it as an act of commital; '*Where I, as a human, fail, you finish.*' I may forget the prayer prayed, but something happened. The seed sown may not germinate now and may pass from our keeping; but '*the commandment came forth*' and somehow, somewhere, God will work out his fulfilment.

In the next stage of my life I remember being largely concerned about prayer for guidance. I went out to Morocco with little real sense of call; I simply went out to help and keep house for my brother who was Medical Director at a Mission hospital and I often wondered whether it was God or my own reasoning that had led me there. I wanted to do his will and it seemed the obvious next step, but did the obvious next step constitute a call from God? I had prayed for a sign or a vision but none had been given. I was very worried indeed.

Then, after a few months, my brother and I drove a young man home to his mountain village. He had been weeks in hospital and had come to follow Christ although later, after being beaten up, he turned back. He pleaded that someone should come to his village, which was the centre of a large tribal area. 'Why should we travel eighty kilometres to hear about Jesus?' he asked.

We stopped for breakfast high up in the foothills and sat, looking out over little hamlets nestling among the rocks. We rested for a time and I read Ezekiel 34.6 '*My sheep wandered through all the mountains and upon every high hill . . . and none did search or seek after them.*' Then I knew, without any doubt, that I was to go up and work in that village. Within six months all the difficulties were resolved: my brother became engaged to be married, a new nurse arrived in the hospital and I was free to go.

All this taught me lessons about guidance that have helped me ever since. I think that God normally guides through circumstances. '*As you go step by step I will open up the way before you,*' should be our normal experience. He does not send signs and visions when the next step seems fairly obvious to our reason and common sense. He leads on, we follow and if we are in doubt, I believe that this prayer is foolproof: '*I want to do your will and this seems right, but if it is wrong, please stop me.*' If an earthly father takes his child somewhere, and the child wants to go with him but accidentally takes a wrong turning, the father will check him and bring him back. Is it likely that the Father of all fatherhood will do less?

But there is another Bible promise which says '*your ears shall hear a word behind you saying, "this is the way, walk in it," when you turn to the right hand, and when you turn to the left.*' I think this means that when God wants us to take some unexpected, unplanned turning, then the voice will be heard and the sign given. Some, at this point, have been led by a clear prophecy or by a dramatic upheaval of their circumstances, but to me it came through a passage in the Bible. When the road ahead is predictable we may travel on step by step, but when the fork in the road comes, the voice will speak clearly. We may sometimes lag behind or run ahead but the Father will not let any child of his, who truly desires his will, miss the way altogether.

I stayed in the mountains for four and a half years doing child welfare work and clinics, until Islamic pressure made my presence a menace to the tiny group of believers, although I often wonder if I gave up too soon. Physically, they were the hardest years of my life; spiritually, they were some of the richest. I sometimes had a companion but I was often alone and then prayer seemed specially easy and intimate, for if God is the only person to whom you can speak in English, you tend to talk often and freely. We saw people turn to Christ, which made it a very joyful time, although later when persecution broke out, very few held on. They were mostly poor, illiterate and ignorant; Christian truth had to be taught them like ABC but faith came naturally. I saw, as I have seldom seen before or since, healings and deliverances in swift, direct answer to prayer, guidance given through dreams and visions. They prayed, as children speak to their parents, about all that concerned them; the sick baby, the strayed goat, the stolen blanket, the unkind mother-in-law, and the need for their daily bread; and God gave them their requests, often in miraculous ways. I was the only one who was ever surprised.

During those years I too came to expect answers like that and, as far as material provision was concerned, I got them every time. But, in other ways, God did not seem to treat me quite as he treated those simple villagers. I knew that we were told to pray as little children and I hoped I was doing so, but I was forgetting that we are also told to grow to maturity. The primary aim of the Christian is to know God and to become like Christ and a new baby 'knows' his mother almost entirely by what she does for him. He takes very little notice of what she says or is, and discipline and correction have little place. He knows her purely through what she gives him and does for him.

But to grow implies a different relationship. The older child begins to listen to what his parents say, and to assess their characters by their behaviour unrelated to himself. To give him everything he asks for instantly would be to spoil him and hinder growth. He learns to understand and accept delayed answers; to trust and be patient. He must also be ready to work for what he wants and sometimes to fight for it.

So it is with prayer. We thank God for the simple receiving of childlike faith, for the prayers asked and answers gladly given; but we need to thank God too for the testings and growth of faith, for the times we have had to say, '*Though he slay me, yet will I trust in him.*' That trust has been founded, not on what he gives, but on what he is. We learn to be thankful too for the times when we have had to rise up in love and obedience and work for the answer to our prayer, or to wrestle against the powers of darkness for the deliverance of a loved one, and sometimes to wait for years and to see him still undelivered. Surely this is all part of the process of maturing.

The next twenty-three years were spent largely at the mission hospital on the coast, with intervals when I came home to nurse my parents. I was in charge of the home for Moroccan student nurses and I also worked among children and babies suffering from malnutrition. There are many happy, grateful memories of those years and they gave me many precious friendships, but there are also memories of extreme pressure and darkness, when the enemy seemed to come in like a flood. Unfortunately, I had never been to a missionary training college and I was not sufficiently prepared for the strength of the attack that is let loose on those who are seeking to challenge Islam with God's truth, nor the gradual disclosure, in the face of it, of the unsuspected depths of pride and selfishness in my own nature. There were times when it seemed as though the devil was blinding my eyes to the great central warfare, by keeping me absorbed in my own private warfare – the struggle to win victory over myself. There were times when I, at least, felt so sunk in weariness and depression that I longed to give up, and prayer became little more than a cry of despair, often uttered in unbelief because surely God would not listen to the prayers of such a failure.

In spite of that, or perhaps because of it, I have come to believe that there is no prayer nearer to the heart of God than the helpless cry of self-despair. The dark tunnel may be a long one, failure reaps its own reward in this life, and sin must be confessed and put away, but it is only when we cry out in the dark 'I can't! please come!' that Christ can really begin to take over. I used to wonder why Jesus said to Peter, '*Satan has desired to have you . . . but I have prayed for you that your faith fail not.*' Why didn't Jesus say '*I have prayed for you that you won't deny me*' and have done with it?

I think it was because the actual denial was not the real moment of crisis. The point where Christ could really take over was the moment of remorse and self-hatred, when Peter went out and wept bitterly, sure that his defeat was the end of everything. That was the point on which Christ's intercessory prayer was focused. It was just there that Peter might either yield to despair for ever or recognise, for the first time, that in him '*dwelt no good thing*', cast himself totally on Christ, and became a new man. The transformed Peter was to become a humble man, who lived the rest of his life marvelling at the grace of God, compassionate, experienced in forgiveness, able to sympathise with others and a faithful and gracious shepherd.

A change comes over our prayer life after we emerge from these tunnels. He brought us through, so we need never despair of anyone else. When I could not pray, he prayed for me; he did not give me up, so he won't give anyone else up, and I need not do so either.

This is the personal side, but there is also another side. Failure and depression in God's service can have terrible, long-lasting

105

results on others and need to be taken seriously. They must be recognised, as I was slow to do, as an oppression and backlash of the evil one, furious at the invasion of his territory, from which there can be deliverance. While I was caught up in my personal spiritual battle, we were blessed by the visit of a Swiss pastor whose main message was spiritual warfare. He taught that the spirit of depression, jealousy, discouragement and weariness could be recognised and cast out in the name of Jesus, provided there was real repentance and confession of sin. From then on we prayed with a fresh understanding of the power and victory of Jesus over evil.

I am now back in England, nursing an invalid aunt, but some day I hope to return to Morocco. My sister from Lebanon has recently joined me, which is a great joy and help. The families of our many nephews and nieces are rapidly increasing and we are getting to know friends on the housing estate where we live, and some of their problems are overwhelming. I find that prayer today is largely concerned with intercession for individuals, a drawing near to God with their needs and a fresh learning to watch and wait for signs of change and growth, believing that roots can be burrowing under the soil long before any shoots appear.

I love my small garden, in spite of being quite unable to keep up with the weeds, but when I plant a seed I do not expect to see a flower blooming within a few days. But there is the excitement of noticing the first tiny sprouting after the watering and the watching, and intercessory prayer seems to me rather like that. We pray and we watch, not necessarily for a transforming miracle, but for the slightest sign of change or spiritual growth. We praise and rejoice over the small green shoot and we water it with our prayers. Keeping a five-year diary has helped me to notice, so often, that there really has been change and spiritual growth in the one prayed for a year ago. Something has happened and will happen as we commit to him the blank pages of the year ahead.

And sometimes, although only occasionally with me, there is the sudden assurance that the prayer has been heard and answered and there is nothing left to do but to wait and watch God at work; to praise him for what he is doing in secret and to be available if necessary. And, of course, we can praise in faith even before the assurance has been given. I love the story of Jehoshaphat going out against that overwhelming army with the singers marching ahead; '*And when they began to sing and to praise . . . the enemy was smitten!*' It fits in well with two lines of a hymn I love:

> '*Glory to Thee for all the grace*
> *I have not tasted yet.*'

In the last three years I have lost two dearly-loved brothers at the ages of sixty-three and fifty-eight, both fathers of large families. Both died of painful, distressing illnesses although earnest, believing prayer was offered up by many people for their healing and through this I have learned more about the prayer of faith. In the past, I think I have wasted a good deal of my time bothering about *my faith*. Had I really got any and was it strong enough to move God to give me what I was asking for? If the project was unlikely to succeed humanly speaking, then I would try and 'work up' my faith. When I was mentally convinced that the answer would be given, I would heave a sigh of relief and feel that I, at least, had done my part. If it was not given in the way I had expected, I just could not understand it. What could have gone wrong?

'Have faith *in God*.' It took me a long time to realise that these mental gymnastics were only efforts to have faith . . . in my faith. Real faith is simply coming to Jesus with our needs and thereby making contact with God. You can make contact with the power house by stretching out your hand and touching the switch, and it does not matter if the hand is small or weak. Jesus talked about little faith, faith as a grain of mustard seed, great faith etc., but he acted alike for all who made contact with him. He responded to the trembling hand of the woman who touched his garment, to the cry of Peter sinking in the waves, just as much as he did to the strong, intelligent certainty of the centurion. Those responses were always right for the individual. Sometimes the healing was immediate, sometimes in two stages. Once there was a delay of four days, at other times it was conditional on the obedience of the suppliant. *They* came, *he* decided.

To have faith in God is to come and know that the love and wisdom of God will decide and act for the best. Once, when I was doing a village clinic in Morocco, a small ragged child crept into the room after everyone else had gone and lay down at my feet. 'What do you want, Sodea?' I asked. She looked and her eyes were bright with fever. 'I'm sick,' she said, 'so I came.' No request, no suggestion, no offer of payment; she lay relaxed and at peace. She had nothing to worry about. She had arrived with her pain and her poverty and was quite sure that I would know what to do. That is faith.

I am learning, increasingly, the value of God's promises in prayer. Some of these promises are highly conditional and need careful self-examination before we can claim them, but some seem to be available to any child of God at any moment of the day. There are decisions to be made; it is good to lay one's hand on James 1 and say, '*Father, you promised me wisdom*,' and to rest in the certainty that we shall be guided. As we get older we are sometimes very tired. Thank God we can sit down for a few moments and rest on Isaiah 40: '*They that wait upon the Lord shall renew their strength*,' to feel that quiet renewal of mind and body and then go on refreshed. I know that there are vast stores of spiritual treasure in the promises of God which I am only just beginning to explore.

For after all, I feel I am still only a beginner in the school of prayer. I am quite busy and although one can practise 'living in the presence of God', I find that some days pass with very little time actually set apart for prayer. Then I know that I have missed the highest and most important ingredient, the source from which all the blessing of the day should flow. I long to learn and practise more but it is a comfort to know that we do not pray alone. Perhaps it is the old, retired Christians who are doing the most for us; some of them spend hours in intercessory prayer. The world considers them out of the running but they can be a centre of power for God. Just before he died, my younger brother, completely disabled by Parkinson's disease and cancer, said to me, 'Isn't it wonderful that, even though I can do nothing else, I can still pray?'

So for that reason, I am not dreading the time when I shall be less physically active. Perhaps then I shall come to know God better than ever before and come closer to the fulfilment of my life-long prayer, '*Lord, teach me to pray.*'

12 Jan Ramsey:
But you Never Asked Me!

Years ago, somebody gave my husband a few words of sound advice. It was during one of his earlier missions in Yorkshire, England, and Vic hadn't been long in the ministry. 'If you want to get on your feet . . . get on your knees!' We have never forgotten those words of wisdom. 'Getting on your knees' is a cliché which we Christians often use, but 'knee drill' is really hard, isn't it? Especially on your knees!

The prayer walk for me has never been easy, and it is a journey I often wish I did not have to make. Life would be so much simpler if we could just wave a magic wand and everything would be all right. Or if we could obtain the desired results without having to be so involved.

My contribution to this book has been as difficult to write as prayer is to experience; both have been one long hard struggle, and I would be dishonest if I led you to believe it had been any other way. On several days I went to my room with the intention of spending time with the Lord, asking him what he wanted me to write, and at the end of the day I hadn't written one word! The interruptions were unbelievable – telephone calls, which nobody else could handle, they just *had* to speak to me and they *had* to have an answer there and then. One of our sheep had died, leaving a week-old lamb which had to be bottle-fed. As I was the only person who knew what to do at the time, I had to go and feed the poor animal, which carried on monotonously bleating for its mother. We hadn't a proper feeding bottle so I had to improvise! And all I wanted to do was to talk to the Lord and get an answer! And I wonder: 'Lord, why on earth do you let these things happen when you know there is a deadline to meet?'

Let me place on record, therefore, that I write this with the confession I am a novice in this business of prayer, that I do not know all the answers and can only write from my own experience. There are still large areas of my life where prayer is still a mystery, because the answers have not yet come. I hold on in faith, believing that God has everything under control.

Being brought up in the Roman Catholic faith and, as a child, attending a convent school, I first experienced prayer as a comforting ritual – my rosary beads were warm and I almost felt that the mother of Jesus was inside each one! I grew up with the subconscious feeling that it was all a matter of 'if I am good, I will go to heaven and perhaps even be an angel!'

Then I experienced the love of Christ in my heart in my late teens and turned my life completely over to him. This brought turmoil in my family, because my mother thought I had lost my mind and insisted I move away from these strange people, who were so fanatical that they made me believe that I was a sinner!

Moving me from my home with my Grandmother in the Midlands to the east coast to be home with my parents only aggravated our family situation because, not long after, I met an evangelist who had come to the town for a crusade, and two years later we were married! (But God really answered prayer, because my dear mother came to know the Lord before she died.)

Marrying a freelance evangelist thrust me into a different lifestyle which meant I had to pray, and pray hard, even if I didn't understand what prayer was about. We 'lived by faith' which means that we were not employed by any organisation and had no regular income, and I had to learn the hard way. Bringing up two small children with a husband who was committed to sharing the Christian faith around the country meant I was often at home without him, having to trust God to supply our needs. In practical terms this was often done through his people, and if they were slow to respond to his prompting, or disobedient, life could be very hard indeed.

In my desperate moments I have asked myself 'Is this all worth while? Is this really the path God wants his children to take?' Non-Christians often seem to have life so much 'easier' in many ways, although I know in my heart that this is just how it appears on the surface. They lack hidden resources which we have available to us – the guidance and encouragement that we can find in God's Word, the love and security of the Christian family and the lifeline of prayer. The problem is that all too often we seem to lack them too! These resources appear to be more like frozen

110

assets than a current account, not because they are unavailable but because we seem to be so bad at drawing on them properly.

From my first days of being a Christian I read lots of books, missionary stories and accounts of those who lived by trusting God – like Rees Howells, Len and Iris Moules, George Mueller, Sister Gemmel and many other heroes and heroines of the Christian church. They have been of tremendous inspiration to me, and as I grew as a Christian I began to understand what wasn't written . . . the agony, the heart searching, the sorrows, misunderstanding and trials of faith that they endured, and to be encouraged to press on. Iris Moules (a missionary with the Worldwide Evangelisation Crusade) will never know the blessing and help that she has been to me in my prayer walk.

Life as a Christian is certainly no soft option. I've had to live too close for comfort at times with a world of turmoil, bitterness and resentment when working for nearly eighteen years with my husband amongst drug addicts. In a small way we tried to wear our Christianity on our sleeves by having them live in our home. During the early days of our work amongst drug abusers we held regular Sunday night meetings close to Soho in London. The basement of a church in Orange Street was our meeting ground.

I'll never forget one night when, alone in the little kitchen washing up the dishes (which always seemed to be one of my regular jobs), a young man came into the room. He slammed the door, got hold of me and held me against it. It terrified me, to say the least. I tried shouting for help, but the words wouldn't come out. I was petrified. This man had a reputation for being violent, especially with women, and I thought the worst. As we stood eye to eye, with his grip getting tighter and a knife to my throat, the name of Jesus came to mind. I attempted several times to say 'Jesus,' but it felt as though the word was locked in my mouth. I seemed to be trapped in this violent embrace, speechless, for hours.

Then suddenly I was able to blurt out the name: 'JESUS! JESUS!' The fellow loosed his grip, pushed me away, ripped open the door and ran off. A very important truth was made real to me that night: The name of Jesus is as powerful as his physical presence. It was just as though Jesus came into that basement kitchen physically the moment I breathed his name. It wasn't just a nice spiritual thought: it was reality. Nothing else could have saved me because the knife was too close.

111

It was a miraculous answer to prayer. I often wish my prayers could be answered so quickly every time! I never enjoy delays. I get frustrated and sometimes discouraged even though underneath, deep down, I know God is working things out. There *is* a strategy in prayer, although understanding it can be difficult.

Trusting God in the practical things of life is one area where faith can falter. Finance has always seemed such a delicate subject to pray about! The work with drug addicts began in our home with twenty-five young people living with us – London's strange society they were called then. Some of them were lesbians, homosexuals, alcoholics, many of whom suffered with what we called 'idle-itis,' and nearly all had diseases of some kind, including veneral disease. I wore myself out trying to look after them all, feeding, clothing and caring for them often acting as a mother figure. One fellow, who called me his 'Mum,' was two years older than I!

It cost a lot more money than we had in those days. In fact, the work started with just ten shillings in the old currency. We lived in Upper Norwood at the time, at the foot of a steep hill. Every day I would have to shop, having just approximately ten shillings – or 50p in today's money – to spend. Then others began to hear of what we were doing and would send gifts of food or money, but it always seemed to be in ten shilling notes at any one time.

I became so tired climbing that hill and one day my prayer was, 'Please, Lord, why don't you send at least a one pound note in one envelope instead of just ten shillings?' So gently, from a feeling deep inside me, came words as though the Lord was answering me: 'But you didn't ask me!' I learned that day to be specific when praying. The Lord loves us to share with him in detail our definite needs. Now I know he could have sent that money at any time, but he wanted me to *ask*. 'Ask and ye shall receive,' the Bible tells us. You may say, 'I've asked, and I haven't received' Luke 11.9. Well, so have I, but we have to pray according to his will, and that is where it is sometimes difficult to decide . . . what is my desire and what is his will?

We saw many miraculous answers to prayer during our eighteen years of working with the drug abusers, but they didn't come easily. I have taken myself apart on many occasions, wondering if there were anything in my life that might be hindering things. There were times when the situation was so desperate and nobody seemed to care, not even God. Heaven was as brass, and the more I would beat upon its doors, the more I would hurt, until eventually I began to realise that with prayer, as in all stages of life, we have to grow up.

Our first relationship with the Father in prayer is, for most of us, like being in a family in the role of a baby, needing a lot of care and attention. Then we develop and eventually go to school to learn the basics of life with lots of teachers to help us on our journey. Adolesence is for some very difficult, both physically and spiritually. We then come to maturity, accepting responsibility for ourselves. We have learned many lessons along the way. It's good to talk our questions over with others but they do not really need to tell us what to do – we *know*. And this is what I think growing up in the Christian walk is all about. Sometimes I talk something over with the Lord, and he doesn't answer, because I know what I should do anyway. I have learned the way, through reading my Bible. I simply have to get on and do it. Obedience matters!

From my limited experience I have discovered that prayer can cease to be effective when we use it as a substitute for obedience to the King of Kings. There are times when the Lord appears to ask foolish things of us and I am left questioning, 'Lord, do we have to go this way? It seems so stupid, so foolish; surely there is a better way, a clearer answer?' But talking to God about it is no substitute for obedience: when we obey, the path is suddenly clear and things happen. Imagine being Joshua! Poor fellow – having to tell the people to walk around the walls of Jericho seven times, and on the seventh time, blow on their horns and the walls will come tumbling down! What foolishness! I wonder how many people reacted that way in their hearts? But Joshua knew God, and the people Joshua. They obeyed and, sure enough, the walls came tumbling down.

I was once talking to a group of ladies in a seminar on Christian growth and made the following statement: 'Prayer can make an honest or dishonest woman of you!' They looked at me in amazement, but then gradually started to nod their heads in warm approval. You see, it is so easy for us to react with 'I'll pray about it,' when asked to be involved in some work or spiritual enterprise. 'I'll pray about it' is a term we Christians often use when we want to avoid an immediate answer to some request. This can make us dishonest because, deep down in our hearts, we know that God wants us to do it, but we are struggling inside, battling against God's will.

Putting out a 'fleece' does not work for me. I remember asking God for guidance about a certain situation years ago, and asking if he would give me a definite sign as he did when Gideon put out his fleece in the book of Judges. The Lord answered me with 'Get on with the job I have given you to do!' and that was the end of fleeces for me. But I know the Lord allows many others to know his will this way, but then, this is *my* path of prayer. There are many occasions, of course, when God *delays* the answer, if delay is the right word, because he knows that it would not be good for us to get our way immediately. Sometimes a delay in getting an answer has meant we were able to obtain a better arrangement, as happened when we came to Kelham.

The trustees of our work had joined us in prayer for a suitable building where we could expand. We had outgrown our existing premises and the ministry was in danger of collapsing because our staff would not be able to cope with the congested conditions much longer. We looked at various properties and many of them seemed just right. One in particular seemed to have everything: it was fully furnished throughout and in mint condition, but we weren't able to raise the money to buy it. Then, out of the blue, the Red House at Kelham, in Nottinghamshire, became available and at the time of writing it is our home and headquarters for the ministry into which the Lord has now brought us. The other building would have been second-best for us. If we had been given our own way, and had the Lord answered our prayers the way *we* wanted them answered, we would not have come to Kelham.

How can I make my prayer life more effective? This question is one that I frequently get asked by others and one which I continually ask myself.

I think it begins with making sure that our lives are lived in line with God's idea of what a Christian life should be like and not just our own. This means that we accept God's forgiveness for all the wrong-doing of the past, thank him for it and then forgive ourselves. Often we find that harder to do than accepting God's forgiveness, and as a result carry round a burden of false guilt. It is not presumption to act as if we're forgiven. The Bible states that Jesus died on our behalf, if we accept that, we *are* forgiven and that settles it. We are free to enjoy that lovely relationship with Jesus which gives us the privilege of sharing our joys and heartaches with him in prayer.

Prayer then becomes several things to us. First, it becomes a life-line between us and God. We have this wonderful 'hot-line' to God called communion. We have a vital link with him which enables us to experience his life in our life. The Bible encourages us to 'pray without ceasing.' This speaks to me of prayer being a lifestyle rather than a special exercise: a continual attitude of the heart and mind, almost as though other activities are incidental to our communion with God. He wants us to have a perfect mature relationship with him . . . all the time, not just in spasms.

From the age of three I was thrust upon the stage and, until my conversion to Christ, every spare moment was devoted to learning a new dance, the lines of a play or practising my singing. It was during my very early days of voice training and voice production that I learned some very basic facts about breath control. Diaphragmatic breathing simply means breathing from the stomach, your innermost being. This is what prayer is to me: breathing in God from the depth of my being; letting Jesus into the depth of my needs; opening up my whole life to him and letting him walk right into my inner self, taking my needs into his hand, walking away with the burdens and replacing them with his answers!

Secondly, prayer becomes a resource to draw upon to help meet the needs of our own lives or the lives of others. As we come into contact *with other people* we can pray for the opportunity to share the claims of Christ with them and we can pray about the things that trouble them.

Thirdly, prayer becomes a channel of praise and worship. It develops into an expression of appreciation and gratitude to God for the things he has done for us.

None of us is bigger than our prayer life. We have the potential to play such a crucial and effective role for God within our homes, communities and even our nation that we must guard against anything or anybody hindering our times of prayer. Reading, talking or even thinking about prayer is *no* substitute for actually praying. That must be a priority, for prayer does change things . . . and people. I have witnessed the power of prayer to heal my sick body. I have seen the evidence of prayer healing other people when all medical hope was gone. There have been numerous occasions, when from a simple attitude of faith, I have prayed for equipment in my kitchen to work again when it was worn out. So I could go on.

My prayer lifestyle has been humorous and serious. It has elated me and made me feel so small. It has baffled me, disappointed me and annoyed me, but I haven't given up although I often wonder why it is that the Lord takes me to the very 'edge' before he answers my prayer. It is like being on the edge of a precipice and I feel I am going to fall over and there is nothing to prevent the fall. I cry out to God, 'Lord, I'm going over . . .' Let me tell you from experience: when you get to *that* place, tie a knot as it were and hang on – underneath are his everlasting arms, and no matter how low you might get, you can never get any lower than his arms! The words of Basilea Schlink, 'Father, I do not understand you . . . but I trust You,' sum up for me the hidden feelings of my heart. Many of the questions remain, but I shall press on in the school of prayer, knowing without a doubt that the Lord cares for me and that I can trust him with my life.

13 Faith Lees:
New Every Morning

Maybe the reason that I have searched for a deeper understanding of prayer relentlessly for the past twenty-five years, is that the first prayer that I prayed with the awareness that I was asking some-one for something, was answered. It was such a shock that I have never recovered, thank goodness! I was twenty-eight years old, happily married with four lively and delightful children. My life had been what I had chosen to make it. For many years I had looked at my decisions carefully and weighed the consequences; nobody could easily persuade me to do anything against my will. I was used to managing my own life with determination and now I was suddenly faced with not knowing what to do!

I didn't exactly *need* to do anything in fact – I only had to discover how to control my thoughts and my feelings. For some unknown reason my emotions seemed to have gone haywire and I couldn't regain my stability. Doctors had tested me all over because I had lost so much weight, but they assured me that I was physically, completely well. For the first time in my life I found myself unable to choose my way ahead, unable to think of anything to do that would make any difference to the way I was feeling.

These were the circumstances surrounding my first prayer: desperation, and no real faith. I prayed very simply, '*God, I can't cope. If it will do any good, come into my life and cope for me*'. Three days later I realised that I was different inside. Something was calm and solid again. I remember lying in the sun, listening to the sea in the distance, watching the clouds, feeling the warmth and smelling the earth and grass under me and realising that the God who was inside me was real and I had to begin to get to know him. The God who had created the world that I could smell, feel and hear, had created peace in me and I didn't know him at all. I was no longer in charge of my own life. This unknown

God, who listened to the first prayer of an insignificant worthless woman, and answered it, was in me somewhere sharing life with me. My choices would never be the same again, I would always need to know what God thought about it! My life and my attitude to life were completely changed.

Einstein once said, *'The important thing is never to stop questioning . . . Never lose a holy curiosity'*. This has been my philosophy in my walk with God. I want to know everything that can be known about him. And I want to know from other people any insights which might open my eyes to great depths of God.

My first questions on prayer were not answered satisfactorily by those around me. So I started reading the writings of the mystics. I was determined to learn from the experiences of those who really know: no one less than a 'Saint' would satisfy me! In fact I am glad that I did go that route, because the humanity of the struggles of those men and women of God enabled me to see myself and my struggle more clearly. The writings of Saint Teresa of Avila and St John of the Cross were so down to earth, open and humble that they became a pattern of how I began to talk to, and approach, God. St Teresa was a woman through and through, and reading her books and autobiography was like entering into her grief at her failures and her joy of her forgiveness, her wonder at God's beauty and her amazement at his love for someone as sinful as her. She drew me into her relationship with God and enabled me to begin to know him for myself. I think that it was through reading these sorts of writings that I realised that my Christian life probably wouldn't be all ease and happiness – that I would have to expect the rough with the smooth, the pain and suffering alongside the freedom and promise of abundant life. I realised that not only would I experience the joy of answered prayers, but would need to know the arid dry wilderness times. I discovered that in all events God was always with me if I was willing to share with him my doubts and fears, failures and my weakness, because I saw that he had been with those who trusted him in that way.

It was a very good thing that I had my children and many good friends to keep my feet on the ground and consistently be a reminder to me that I wasn't a saint with a capital 'S' – nor had I the time to meditate and contemplate as much as I longed to do. I had to stay in the tension of life and make sure that my experience of God became a lived out reality. I used to cry out to God to enable me to tell everyone about him and he would direct me back to loving my children and my family. He seemed to be more concerned with the reality of my ability to love, than with my desire to talk about him! I found life very constricting at times, and yet God never changed his words to me.

When I began to pray, to learn about God and myself, my first questions were, was I talking to thin air or was God really listening? I fairly quickly decided that I would go crazy if I went on holding a conversation with someone I didn't believe was there! In John 4.24 Jesus says to the woman at the well, '*God is spirit, and those who worship him must worship him in spirit and in truth*'(- reality - Amp. version). As I began to talk to God and question my life with him, I was conscious of his Spirit within me either struggling with, or encouraging, my spirit. Our conversations were often shouts and cries from me and gentle honesty from him, but they always brought me peace in the end.

The years when the children were young were when I learnt how to share my heart and my longing with God. I began to find out from him his ways of going about life and his views about people. He often used to correct my critical and selfish views, and made me realise how I expected everything to be on my terms. Certainly my ways were often not his ways, but it was not difficult to feel the difference between walking in his way and in my way – it was the difference between darkness and light – the difference that I knew deep down within me, between before I asked God into my life and after.

I discovered through prayer that God's ways always led towards reconciliation and unity. I came to know the truth of a saying of St Bernard, *Nothing can work me damage, except myself. I am a real sufferer by my fault*! And that was coupled with an old adage that my mother had pressed home to me: *You can only put your own side right*. It was a time of learning of God's love and forgiveness first-hand as I struggled to change my attitudes and impatient temperament. At times I would discover that my spirit was feeling thin and pinched and I usually realised that I was holding on to a critical attitude and was full of judgement. It was at those moments, as I struggled in prayer, often in the night, that I discovered that God had a totally different view of people to mine, and that I neeeded to see them the way that he did. There was hardly a night or day when I didn't have to ask his forgiveness for my lack of love.

119

I remember the blinding flash of understanding I had when I realised the significance of Matthew 6.14–15 where Jesus says, *For if you forgive men their sins, your heavenly Father also will forgive you, but if you do not forgive men their sins, neither will your Father forgive your sins*. I suddenly understood that any unforgiveness and bitterness in me could and did separate me from God. I had at times spent hours, even months, praying from an angry self-righteous heart which had been a complete waste of time. Since then I have always searched my heart and asked God to search it in case I have any hardness against anyone before I start to pray. God loves to help me forgive others, so he doesn't hesitate to point out where I need to get busy!

When the disciples wanted to know how to pray they asked Jesus to teach them (Luke 11.1). When I started to learn to pray I did the same, and still do when I am praying for someone and don't know exactly how to pray. Jesus is interceding always for us and can show us how to intecede for those we love, and for these we don't love. He is always with us to open our understanding on how to love and how to pray. There is never a time when I feel that I have fully learnt how to pray, but it is always possible to ask. To know *how*, *when*, *what* and *who* to ask are a vital aspect of prayer.

In Proverbs 2 3–5 it says, *Yes, if you cry out for insight and raise your voice for understanding, if you seek it like silver and search for it as hidden treasures; then you will understand the fear of the Lord and find the knowledge of God*. And St Paul says in 1 Corinthians 9–10, *What no eye has seen, nor ear heard, nor the heart of man conceived, what God has prepared for those who love him, God has revealed to us through the Spirit. For the Spirit searches everything, even the depths of God*. Verses like these drive me to search and pray for deeper and deeper knowledge of God. In addition, the knowledge that I have the Holy Spirit within me to pray with me and through me is a constant wonder and strength.

Jesus said, *When the Spirit of truth comes, he will guide you into all truth* (John 16.13); and it is this dimension of my life with God that I am still discovering. The first time (many years ago) that I consciously realised that I had insight into a situation beyond my own knowledge, and that because of this wisdom and understanding, the couple that I was praying for and trying to help began to listen to me and do what I said, I was extremely frightened. At that time I had no comprehension of the Holy Spirit, I did not know who he was; all I knew was an incredible joy and deepened love for God and for these friends.

Since those days the Holy Spirit has been with my husband Tom and me, helping us to follow Jesus more and more fully. It is quite true that the Holy Spirit takes us into all truth. To begin with he took us into a position of trust in God beyond anything we had experienced before. He brought people to our home to be healed physically. In addition he brought people who had never been loved and needed to know love. He gave us faith in God's faithfulness, and longing to share our faith with those who had none. He has also taken us into the truth about ourselves and shown us depths of anger and fear which we never knew we had. He has helped us rid ourselves of the negative attitudes which separate us from those we should be loving.

Over the years I have prayed in various ways. Probably the most important discovery was the finding of what I call my own 'rhythm' By this I mean, the way of praying and relating to God that meets my needs as an individual. None of us are alike, we each have our own way of relating to people and to God. I tend to be a person who dislikes to feel separation and consequently l like to be in touch with God all the time. I like to know where I am and what is going on. One advantage of my life in a community is that others can also help me to know myself. If I seemed scattered or harassed or short-tempered, those I live with will notice it well before I realise it myself. Any of those unpeaceful states is an indication to me that I need to pay attention to my 'rhythm'.

Obviously to find a stability in prayer one must spend enough time reading and thinking about God, because he is the other person in the relationship! God is a God of compassion and feeling, so it is important to know what hurts him and what pleases him, what makes him angry and what arouses his compassion. It is hard to comprehend that the power and might which created the universe is tenderly and intimately involved with each one of us from the moment of conception. I know I find this difficult to grasp. Therefore part of my 'rhythm' is to spend enough time meditating on who God is, and I am grateful that I learnt how to be still and to meditate when I first started to pray years ago.

Meditation is often thought to be only a part of the Eastern religions but it is also, or should be, part of our Christian heritage.

It simply means taking time to learn how to still your mind and emotions and how to centre yourself on God. Meditating is such a part of my life that I find it hard to read my Bible without doing it; but far more helpful still is for me to put aside sufficient time to purposefully meditate on different aspects of God.

During these times I bring my thoughts in line with God's, and can then begin to see their relevance to my own life. To do this while having inner stillness is a means of adjusting our preconceived, long-set, view points, conditioned by the past, to God's perspectives. And this in turn creates an enduring peace within our being.

Meditation and contemplation may go together as I take time with God, but for me they serve very different purposes. For me, meditation serves to bring peace to my mind, and through that, to my spirit, while contemplation takes place when my emotions and feelings are engaged with God. Meditation can lead me to contemplation, when I wonder in adoration at God and his love, but more often my feelings come to a unity with him through some form of pain felt deep within.

Sometimes it could be the pain of my own separation (through anger or a different point of view) from one of these close to me, which enables me to contemplate God's pain at his separation from his world. If I feel such excruciating pain at so small a rift with one other person, I can realise in a minute way what God must feel. As I pray for those around me who don't know God, and therefore have no way to make sense of their lives, I can contemplate and feel the pain within them and know God's longing to be known by them. Few things are more painful than to love someone who rejects, ignores or is unaware of, your love. This has been my experience as people have come to find healing at Post Green. The pain of their frightened rejection of love has helped me to find unity with God. As I have wept with my pain and their pain I have understood God's pain and his comfort. St Paul says in 2 Cor 1.5, *For as we share abundantly in Christ's sufferings, so through Christ we share abundantly in comfort too*. I know this to be true as I enter into God's suffering in my prayer life.

There are two other ways in which I pray and possibly they are my most constant and consistent communication with God. The first was taught me years ago by a very dear friend called Edgar Trout. He was a man of mighty faith and he shared with us his life with God and what he had learned from God. He used what he called 'arrow prayers' and they were instant cries for insight and help. I honestly don't know what I would do if I hadn't learnt in this way how to ask and receive and believe. Each day is full of situations which need wisdom and insight usually beyond my own abilities and knowledge. It is exciting to walk through it in communion with God.

The second is something I discovered for myself, although I am sure that other people have made the same discovery. I call it my 'heart prayer' and it is rather like the 'Jesus Prayer' of the Orthodox Church, '*Lord Jesus Christ Son of the Living God, have mercy on me, a sinner*'. In fact I sometimes use the 'Jesus Prayer', but more often I find myself praying more about my own particular heart attitude of the moment. My prayer could be, '*Lord, may my heart be filled with your love*' or '*Lord, keep my heart open to hear you*' or '*Lord, let your love be ever in me*'. They are repetitive prayers which seem to issue out of my heart as the need arises, which is most of the time!

As I grow older I find more and more excitement about God. Every day my knowledge of his love is strengthened by experiencing his love. It is the way Isaiah puts it in chapter 26.3:

'*You keep him in perfect peace, whose mind is stayed on you, because he trusts in you.*'

14 Margaret Cundiff:
Prayer . . . and Me

'. . . And thank you Lord for bringing us safely to the end of this day.' As my husband Peter prayed those words we heard the sound of galloping feet up the stairs, the banging of doors, and then our bedroom door burst open. 'Come quickly, Alison's ceiling is coming in!' shouted our son Julian. We dived out of bed, rushed into Alison's bedroom to find water pouring from the ceiling. Fortunately our daughter Alison was elsewhere. Soon we discovered the source of the trouble, Julian climbed into the roof and stopped the offending pipe, and after a good deal of hard work mopping up, we got back to bed in the early hours of the next morning.

As we prepared for bed the following night – or rather at the end of the same day, I looked at the clock: 11.55 pm. 'I think we'll wait until after midnight, before we thank God for bringing us safely to the end of the day', I said so we waited solemnly until the hands had passed the hour of twelve, before giving thanks to God.

Perhaps this sounds an odd way of approaching prayer, but at least it's honest! When Peter and I were married, the friend who married us, a wise vicar, gave us some very good advice. 'Never go to sleep before you resolve any difficulties you may have had with each other during the day. Be sure you will have your ups and downs, but don't take the downs into the next day and never go to sleep before you have put the day into God's hands, and yourselves into his safe keeping. Make sure you pray together even if it's only to pray the Lord's prayer.' Good advice indeed, – be right with each other and be right with God'. Does it work? Well, it has done for over twenty-four years and so we have no reason to think it will fail us in the future. Perhaps one day as an old 'Darby and Joan' we will be interviewed and asked for our secret of a happy married life – well *there's* the secret now.

As our children came along we prayed with them each night, but as they grew up we realised that they were people in their own right, and the time had come for them to have the privacy to pray – or not to pray – without us being there. This came home strongly to me one night after our son had shot down to the bottom of his bed and mumbled away his prayers. Sternly I said, 'come up here and say them again.' With wide eyes and a knowing grin he said, 'Actually they were not addressed to you!' – the message was received and understood.

But of course we pray for our children every day, we commit them to God and leave them with him.

What we do though is always to say Grace at meals. We take it in turns and it is simply saying 'thank you' to God for providing for us. Our children do so without embarrassment even in the presence of their friends or visitors to our home. It is part of our life together, like eating, talking, sharing. It's as matter of fact as saying 'please', 'thank you' and 'sorry' to each other, for God is part of our family.

It has been said 'the family that prays together stays together' and I believe that the very simple action of saying thank you to God at mealtimes is something that binds us together, as a family and something that hopefully our children will take with them when they have homes and families of their own.

Yes, there is prayer in the family situation together, and prayer together in the family of the church. It is important we pray together as God's family the church, not just in Sunday services in the more formal setting, but in the informal meeting, the home groups and clubs. Sadly the old fashioned 'Prayer Meeting' seems to have disappeared from many churches, less and less people attend and so they have been replaced by other things. I am sorry about this trend, for I do believe the prayer meeting is the power house of the church. Let's get back to the prayer meeting even if it is only a small one, for the promise of Jesus is *where two or three are gathered together in my name there am I in the midst.* I'm sure it would prove the answer to many of the problems congregations are experiencing, and would revitalise and renew the life and work. Prayer is never a waste of time!

Of course a prayer meeting doesn't have to be on a big scale, organised regularly. What about those times we meet one another in our homes for a 'cuppa', dropping in for half an hour, calling to discuss something? Why not use some of this time to talk to the Lord as well as talk to each other? We talk to each other about so many things, get excited, moan, rejoice, ask for help from each other – why not turn those things over to the Lord? We could find that it helps more than anything we could do.

When I was asked to say something about prayer and my own prayer life it was quite a challenge, for it has meant I have had to sit down and look at my life from the perspective of prayer – and what an untidy scene it is. I would have liked to have been able to say how ordered it all is, how disciplined, how easy, but instead I must admit to being erratic and undisciplined. Many times it seems dry and dull, and yet I also can say what a marvellous experience prayer is, in spite of me!

As I have grown older, the ordered form of worship has become increasingly dear to me. As I come to the Communion Service – and I must confess particularly when it is the 1662 Holy Communion service – I know I am no longer alone in my praying, I am borne along *'with angels and archangels and with all the company of heaven,'* lauding and magnifying *'Thy glorious name, evermore praising Thee and saying, Holy, Holy, Holy, Lord God of hosts, heaven and earth are full of Thy glory, glory be to thee, O Lord most high . . .'* (*Book of Common Prayer*). That prayer never ceases to fill me afresh with a sense of being part of that company in heaven and on earth. I experience in part something of the joy of heaven, knowing my oneness with the Christian family and with God himself. It has never lost its wonder nor its joy, and in fact grows each time I join in those words. Some would say 'familiarity breeds contempt' but, for me familiarity has bred a sense of freedom in the spirit, when I feel like a bird soaring upward, absolutely free. I long for time to stand still, to remain in that joyous experience of being caught up into God. However, like the disciples on the mountain I have to come down, down to the everyday world, yet as I do so I know I have been renewed by God for service. I find this specially so as the time comes to share in the bread and the wine. As I administer the chalice and see those people coming with hands outstretched I am so thankful for the privilege of ministry – of being able to serve others and share the good things of God with them.

Yes, there is the joy in worshipping together. There is also the strengthening that comes through times of quiet, all alone in church. I know one can pray anywhere, but in church I find the atmosphere is right; somehow the walls are soaked with the prayer of people, so many people, there is a sense of prayerfulness and that helps the pray-er. I can understand the people of old who sought sanctuary in church – and found it. I find sanctuary in church, not because I am on the run from the law – but because I am often on the run from the world, from pressure, from demands, from myself. Sometimes life just builds up, I feel caught in a web of 'doing' and activity and then – I know where to run!

Our church in Selby is not all that old by most standards, for it was only built at the turn of the nineteenth century. When I first came into it I thought it rather dull, dark and drab, but I have come to love it and over the last few years it has been brightened considerably through cleaning, new carpets, and the effort of so many. But there is more to it than that: it is my 'home' – the place where so much has happened *to* me, and *in* me. I feel safe, loved, protected. I have been in there alone when the bright sun has danced through the windows, making the church light and warm. I have sat alone when outside the storms have raged, with the rain belting down. I have even sat there in the dark – and yet never alone, how could I be? I have known the power and the presence of the Lord – and like a child relaxed and safe in the arms of its mother, I have been at peace. Prayer for me is being with God, in his presence, letting go of all the worries, the demands, just dropping them off like discarded clothes.

Don't get the idea I do most of my praying in church though, for in comparison to the time when I can be either taking part in public worship, or in church on my own, most of my time is spent very much in the world at large. I live in a noisy world, full of sound, action, business. I charge through life, shopping bag on one arm, clutching my Uher tape recorder and microphone, note-book and tape boxes sticking out of my pockets, with the leads, wires, and all the paraphernalia of a housewife cum broadcaster cum deaconess cum a thousand and one things. My prayers are often said very much on the run, between the supermarket and the studio, between cutting up the vegetables for lunch to editing tape for tomorrow's programme. I've tried to analyse my praying and I've come to the conclusion that it comes under three head-ings. 'Lord, I think you are absolutely marvellous, thank you, thank you, thank you.' 'Oh Lord, I am so sorry . . .' and 'Lord, I really think I could do it better than you . . .' One things just leads to another, for as I praise and thank him I realise just what a mess I am making of life, how much I fail to reach even my own standards, leave alone his . . . and then so often I question what he is doing, and how he is doing it, I begin to feel I could make a much better job of running the world, dealing with a situation, even sorting out that difficult person I met this morning . . . and then I fall flat on my face, I have to shout 'help' and then thank God, he is there!

– I don't learn, not even by my own mistakes, the cycle goes round and round and round! Yet I take heart it's not just me, I only have to read the psalms to see the psalmist had the same sort of trouble! He praises, confesses AND complains, but at least he is honest with God, and I believe that is important. I've long ago given up trying to play games with God, it just doesn't work – after all he knows me better than I know myself, I can't pull the wool over his eyes, pretend to be someone I'm not – and I'm just grateful he doesn't give up on me. He goes on chipping away, doing a bit of moulding, rubbing off the sharp edges – one day he may make me quite presentable – by his grace.

Sometimes I feel dry and tired, the last thing I want to do is pray. I find at these times I do what in north country jargon is called 'mooch' – I wander around, rather aimlessly, finding silly things to be occupied with, but actually doing nothing. It takes a lot of effort to make myself stop, sit down and relax. It takes more effort to open my Bible and let God speak to me, as I am. It's at these times I find the psalms so helpful and I like to read them aloud, slowly, deliberately. As I do I feel the tension ebbing away, I begin to slow down, take my concentration off myself and my concerns and absorb myself into the mood and feelings of those words. I think particularly of psalms like the 139th: '*Whither shall I go from your spirit, or whither shall I flee from your presence? . . . even the darkness is not dark to you, the night is bright as the day, for darkness is as light with you . . .*' Or like the 51st, '*Create in me a clean heart O God, and put a new and right spirit within me. Cast me not away from your presence, and take not your Holy Spirit from me, restore to me the joy of your salvation, and uphold me with a willing spirit.*'

I let the words roll over me like the waves of the sea, I bathe in them, allow them to take me where they will, I close my eyes, relax my body and give myself space. Thanksgiving just flows naturally then. I want to thank God, I want to praise him, I want to be with him. Then I turn and look at my life, what's going on, what I am involved in. The people, the relationships, and this can often be a dreadful shock, seeing the pettiness of my life, the stupid things I do, the way I ride roughshod over other people, my attitudes, my behaviour, and what can I say but 'Forgive me . . . I'm sorry . . .' Yes, I know I am forgiven, I know he loves me, but I need to tell him, I need to express it in words, because otherwise I can go on making excuses to myself, being blind to my sin, yes, sin. It can be painful, as the biting coldness of the sea, the sting and slap of the waves on the skin can be, but it is necessary. I find it helpful, three or four times a year, to spend some time with a trusted and godly minister and share with him what is going on in my life, spread it out, and accept his guidance and counsel. We can blind ourselves to what is actually happening in our lives and it's good to have someone to share with. Not dashing around here and there, trying out various people in the hope that one will give us the advice we would like to hear, but being ready to listen and be guided and helped by someone who is wiser than ourselves. It's quite biblical, reading the epistle of James will assure you of that fact!

When I was asked to contribute to this book and share my experience on the 'path of prayer' I told a friend and colleague of mine, David. He smiled at me and said 'Yes, it's a bit of a stony path at times isn't it love?' for he shares with me very much in my times of exhilaration and frustration – he knows me pretty well! Yes, it *is* a stony path at times, uneven, rough. There are times when it's like bouncing along on velvet green turf, when the view is spectacular, the way ahead clear and bright; but there are many times also when cloud obscures even the next step . . . yet it is a path, and it is leading in the right direction!

A road that is dead straight, even, open and predictable, would be . . . boring! I may have many ups and downs on my path of prayer, I get myself into the most amazing situations but I am on the right path and it's very exciting!

Yes, prayer can be a most wonderful experience – even when the water does come through the ceiling, or I'm 'mooching' around convinced I have the troubles of the world on my shoulders. It is wonderful when I am sharing in the feast of feasts, the Holy Communion service, times when I'm completely at one with God in the peace of our church or out in the 'highways and byways' of North Yorkshire on my way to get an inverview for the breakfast show.

I wonder what God thinks of my prayers. I would like to think it's rather as I feel when the phone rings and I pick it up and a voice the other end says, 'Hello Mum, it's me . . .' I know it's one of my children, and I just say 'hello, love' – and I listen. I don't think it is wrong to imagine that when I say to God 'Hello father, it's me! He smiles, inclines his ear and says 'hello, love,' . . . and one day it will be even more than that, it will be, 'Welcome home – come and join the rest of the family, it's good to have you home at last.'

'Surely goodness and mercy
shall follow me all
the days of my life and
I shall dwell in the
house of the Lord for ever.'

(Psalm 23.6)

15 Sue Barnett:
Anytime, Everywhere

Our Christmas had been a good one. There had been time for family, friends, conversations, leisurely meals and moments to catch our breath after an eventful year. The early days of the new year saw our home return to some form of normality and brought the first visit of the dustmen. I handed them my last sack of rubbish and turned to enter my strangely bare hall, stripped of decoration and holly. The dustman called out to me. 'Hey love! Shall I take those?' He was pointing to the two sprigs of artificial holly and a lonely Christmas rose lying on the doormat. 'No!' I laughed 'They're not real – I might need them next year!'. That Christmas spray is etched on my memory and the seemingly insignificant conversation with the friendly refuse collector keeps echoing in my mind. I am reminded of how prayer used to be. It looked effective enough. I used it for a while, then either discarded it, or packed it away in case I might need it again in the future. The idea of praying was familiar to me. It cropped up on occasions like holly at Christmas and then was forgotten. I went through the motions, learned from a loving family, and at the age of eleven came to know Jesus personally. But my prayers stayed in the parrot fashion era of childhood, and too often prayer lay discarded and lifeless on the doormat of my life.

As a baby has to grow physically and learn to communicate with his father and mother, so we must grow spiritually and learn to communicate with our heavenly father. We must progress from those initial infant cries for attention, if we are to experience the excitement and adventure of a continuous, two-way, living conversation and relationship with God. How have Stephen and Duncan, my two teenage sons, acquired adult conversation, that on occasions leaves me speechless? Through a continuously developing relationship with their parents. In their early years they were always with me. I cuddled them, talked to them, laughed with them and at times scolded them. My evangelist husband, Doug, was frequently away on missions, so I shared everything with them. As I did so I discovered just how much a child responds to, and is capable of, communication. God is longing to show us how much we are capable of, by his Holy Spirit, in and through prayer. As an ordinary mum I lack maturity of judgement and wisdom, at times, in talking with my teenagers, but in prayer we have a Father who has perfect wisdom, patience and understanding. The more we spend time with him, the more we will know these words by E M Bounds to be true: *'Prayer is a way of life, life is a way of prayer'*. They are now becoming a living reality as I am learning that prayer is an attitude of life as well as special daily acts in my life.

The disciples who spent so much time with Jesus on this earth, saw the power and impact of his perfect life. It was dynamite! As a result did they ask him for training in preaching techniques with the masses, in storm control on Galilee, or in healing the sick? Rather, as they quietly observed his life, they pinpointed the source: *'Lord, teach us to pray.'* That simple request led to teaching about prayer that equipped the disciples for a tough future, when without communication with God, they would have collapsed. It has held the key down through the centuries to living life to the full – continous consultation with the person who gave us that life in the first place. He knows our limitations and frustrations, and can help us cope with them. He sees our potential and wants to fulfil it in us. My discovery of prayer as a vital experience began when I joined the ranks of these disciples who made these words their own:*'Lord teach me to pray'* That is a prayer which God delights to answer and I find that I am being led into four basic areas of practice, although I have know the theory for years.

First, I have learnt the need to be *simple*. This shouldn't be too hard a lesson to learn but – what a tangled web we weave in prayer! My motives, attitudes, hopes and fears can all complicate my approach to God. The following words are a great help to me:

'Jesus take me as I am,
I can come no other way,
Take me deeper into you.
Make my flesh life melt away.
Make me like a precious stone,
Crystal clear and finely honed.

Life of Jesus shining through,
Giving glory back to you.'

I need to be honest and straightforward in my approach to God and expect answers. That 'fine honing' can be painful but it is necessary! I am learning not to beat about the bush and to come straight to the point. It is such a shame that so often only pain, tragedy or disaster brings the directness in prayer that God longs for.

At the age of six I thought that the height of maturity was to stand at an ironing board and press the creases out of a mountain of washing. Today a basket full of shirts turns that dream into a nightmare! However I longed in those early days to iron the handkerchiefs. The opportunity came and my mother left me in charge. I finished, and with great care unplugged the iron and stood it to cool. I then decided to continue in my mother's footsteps in swiftly banging the board into its folded position. I had admired her dexterity in this glorious thumping event and couldn't wait to 'have a go'. My six year-old fingers were placed at one end and then slightly tilting the board, I gave the other end a tremendous thump! I remember to this day the pain that followed. The heavy old board crushed my fingers, and all I could do was literally gasp for help – a simple cry of agony! My mother heard it and hurtled downstairs to release me. The original meaning of Hebrews 2 verse 18 is, *God is able to 'run to the cry' of his children*. I am slowly learning to be as simple and direct in my appreciation, praise and confession as I am in my urgent cries for help.

My childhood prayers were regularly closed with 'God bless all the people all over the world, and Timmy the cat!' I was specific enough about the cat who mattered to me, but the 'rest of the world' was beyond my comprehension. God gives attention to detail. The Bible assures me that he knows my name (Isaiah 43.1) and every facet of my nature (Jeremiah 1.5). He knows me intimately and I need to take time to get to know him, so I can be *specific* in my praise of who he is as well as what he does when I need help I read the Psalms, especially Psalm 103. When vagueness creeps into prayer it paralyses it. Just as 'world' in my childhood prayers covered a multitude of people, so the word 'sin' covers literally a multitude of sins. I need the discipline of keeping short accounts and confessing specific sins so that God can cleanse my mind and heart. Any fuzziness in the use of the word 'sin' can lead to unconfessed hurt, misunderstanding, and bitterness. I am continually challenged by a translation from the Chinese, of Psalm 139. 23–24:

> 'Oh God examine me (as in the customs). Test my inmost thoughts, intentions and meanings. Look right inside me (X-ray me) and see if there is hate, evil in my being. You may take my hand along the heavenly way.'

Taking this as my own prayer, I wrote down those inmost thoughts, intentions, and meanings. As the X-ray eye of God rooted out the specific hate and evil, and made me confront them in the cold print, I realised afresh the gift of forgiveness. After confessing each specific sin, I determined that tearing up that sheet of paper was not sufficient. I burnt it and rejoiced that God remembers those sins no more and will help me fight them in the future.

To be *specific* in prayer, I have developed a weekly prayer diary. Each page is headed with the day and the week and contains the names of people and the situations that I am committed to pray for regularly. As items arise for prayer, I add them to the appropriate day with comments when God answers prayer. To look back over the diary is a constant encouragement, and raises the expectation level of my faith as I see what God has done in lives and circumstances.

Activity and impulsiveness are marks of my character, and to sit for any length of time capturing my thoughts on paper is difficult. The other day as I was working on this chapter, I dropped everything and on the spur of the moment headed for the beach and the pounding surf, to catch a breath of fresh air. It is said that we can speak to God at any time or place, but do I take advantage of this wonderful opportunity: through my impulsive nature, God is teaching me not only to be disciplined in prayer, but also to be *spontaneous* in prayer. He is enabling me to have an awareness of him in all situations. As I walked, dodging the spray, tossed up by the windswept sea, I filled my lungs with clear, salty air. The sharp breeze cleared my mind, and my muddled thoughts started tumbling out to the one person who understands me completely. Ahead, the coast swept on to Poole and Swanage, while Hengistbury Head faded in the storm clouds – and not a soul in sight. Yet, I wasn't alone. Just as Jesus walked by the sea with his disciples, he walked with me, listening to my hopes, fears and concerns. There is a time for systematic communication with God, but if I always waited until I am organised I would never make it! We don't tell our children not to talk to us until they are grammatically perfect in their English. Their verbal stumblings are interpreted by a loving and understanding parent, who is delighted by the fragile attempt at communication, because it enables a relationship to be developed and deepened. God understands our varying temperaments and weaknesses and longs to hear from us *however* we feel. Those walks by the sea are a breath of fresh air to my mind, body and spirit. Here I can freely share with God those things that are on my heart. Without interruption, I can voice my thoughts and sing those hymns and choruses that are direct prayers:

> '*I love you Lord and I lift my voice*
> *To worship you, O, my soul rejoice!*
> *Take joy my King in what you hear;*
> *Let it be a sweet, sweet sound in your ear.*'

Mingled with the roar of the wind and thunder of the sea, my voice is not drowned out because God longs to hear from me, his child!

To be accompanied on a long car journey, helps time to pass quickly. Interesting conversation, and lively discussion keeps me alert, and my concentration improves. As driving time increases in my life and work, I find it valuable for prayer, and great for spontaneity in sharing with God. Travelling through hills, villages or towns, God uses the kaleidescope of life I am seeing, to spur me on to pray. Stopping for children racing for school, reminds me of those I know at home concerned for exams or football matches, teachers and students. An ambulance, the postman, birds following a lone tractor, or roadworks, all can trigger off a train of thought which becomes prayer when shared aloud or silently with my unseen passenger. I love starting the day driving through silent darkened roads, as the sun rises and the traffic multiplies. The wakening world, whether crisp with frost or dren-

137

ched with rain, speaks of God's love and care and can draw from my heart spontaneous thanks and praise.

Much of my childhood was spent standing on my head! I could never sit still or wait patiently. With exception to the headstands, this still holds true. I would rather 'get up and go', than observe from the sidelines. Fourteen years ago it was Duncan's first visit to the dentist. It is still very clear in my memory. The dentist was extremely patient and understanding as he built up the toddler's confidence in him. The dental chair became an aeroplane and Duncan pressed every button in sight. Different sounding instruments were put into action and multi-coloured mouth washes sampled. As the two year-old grew weary he sank back into the leather chair. With a sigh of relief, the dentist said, 'OK' son. Lets be still. Open up and I'll take care of these teeth.'

I have discovered that my spontaneity in prayer, if not controlled by God, can lead to a frantic striving to solve the problems myself. Just as Duncan had to be still to allow the expert to deal with a problem tooth, so I am learning to be *still* in God's company. To enjoy his presence and listen to his voice. To open up my life for his touch of encouragment, correction or challenge.

Many of the 'gods' worshipped today, from pop stars to sportsmen, welcome plenty of noise and applause in adoration of them. As the screaming mounts and the drums roll, I am reminded of the contrasting entrance God made to this world, clothed as man in Christ Jesus. Throughout his comparatively short life on this earth, he frequently shrank from the crowds and the attention of his followers, to spend time alone in communication with his father. His disciples were encouraged in the same practice when he invited them to join him:
'*Come with me by yourselves to a quiet place and get some rest.*' (Mark 6.31) In my crowded day to day living, I am learning to answer swiftly that command, '*Be still and know that I am God.*' (Psalm 46.10)

I have built more deep, lasting relationships in our weekly church Keep Fit group, in the last five years, than at any other time in my life. We enjoy the sixty minutes of exercise but it is interesting to note that the most difficult exercise for most people to do, is to relax and be still. It has to be worked at and practised. The same goes for that spiritual stillness which will always lead to more effective action.

From the words of Psalm 46.10 above, I can see why the Good

News version says, '*Stop fighting . . . and know that I am God*'! At the age of eleven years, a battle was raging in my heart and life against a name that was disturbing me. The word Jesus had been familiar to me all my life. I had sung it and read it, but now suddenly it embarrassed me and scared me! I can remember a similar experience in my earlier years when, with a father away during the war, 'Daddy' had only been a name and a black and white photograph. The problem arose when in 1945, I discovered he was more than just a name! He was a strapping six footer, who said he loved me and came to live in my house. It took some getting used to! The struggle I was having at eleven was with the growing awareness that Jesus was more than just a name, more than a baby in a manger. He was a living person! The Son of God, who was demanding the central place in my life. I must either accept him or reject him. The prayer that changed the whole direction of my life was stark in its simplicity; I don't remember the words, I just remember a 'Cease Fire'! God said 'stop fighting', and I did. In the stillness, I knew he had come into my life.

The years passed and I stood at the kitchen sink, elbow deep in soap suds and nappies. My two boys were sleeping. As I stood looking across the toy-strewn lawn, I poured out my pent-up feelings to God who had stuck with me through thick and thin! I felt tired, inadequate and useless. Again God spoke through that verse: '*Be still, stop fighting!*' My struggle was with the mundane tasks which seemed never ending. I was kicking against domesticity, and feeling hopelessly trapped. The words first spoken to the blind man in Luke 18.40, God now spoke right into my kitchen. '*What do you want me to do for you?*' Like a child, I didn't really know, and I told him so. 'I just want to be useful, please show me what I can do.' In direct answer to that prayer, God took the very home and circumstances in which I felt so stifled and exhausted and opened it up for fresh opportunities in introducing friends and neighbours to the personal God I had met so many years before.

Prayer is an individual, personal experience, but the one prayer often on my lips and in my heart today is best expressed in the words written by Graham Kendrick:

Restore O Lord
The honour of your name

In works of sovereign power,
Come shake the earth again
That men may see
And come with reverent fear
To the living God
Whose Kingdom shall outlast the years.

ii Restore O Lord
In all the earth your fame
And in our time revive
The Church that bears your name
And in your anger
Lord remember mercy
Oh living God
Whose mercy shall outlast the years.

iii Bend us O Lord
Where we are hard and cold
In your refiner's fire
Come purify the gold
Though suffering comes
And evil crouches near
Still our living God
Is reigning, He is reigning here.

16 Meryl Doney:
Give up 'Giving up'!

Some nights, when we've put the kids to bed, read them a story and settled both of them in their bunks, Ellie says, 'I don't want to pray tonight.' Other evenings she'll talk about the day, volunteer things to say thank you for and even come up with some revealing items to say sorry about! And once or twice she's brought a tear to my eye with a sweet rendering of the school going-home-prayer in song. Ellie is now six and Lewis, her brother, four and already they are learning about prayer.

As I thank God for them both, yet again, I realise that it is now six years since I had any real time to myself. I suppose children come as a shock to most new parents. Although they try, veteran mothers and fathers can't really convey the work they will involve, the responsibility and worry and the sheer amount of time they take up.

If you have been used to planning your own time and being a fairly free agent, they come as a sudden and unwarranted intrusion. If you really rather like your own company and quiet solitary pursuits like reading, it is very difficult to get used to being in the company of another individual, night and day, with absolutely no let up. Not to mention that small person being totally dependent upon you for a large part of the time. Put all this together with the tiredness, and the shock is complete.

Now none of this is new to anyone who is a parent, but it was new to us when we had Ellie. That it didn't throw us completely is due mostly to the fact that my husband Malcolm and I worked at it together; to the support of the church, good health and generally even tempered natures. How people manage, who have to cope without most of these, I do not know.

One of the main casualties in all this, as far as I was concerned, was my prayer life. I was converted at the age of seventeen, having been a member of my local Anglican church all my life.

Our family were regular church goers and as I grew up, it was my whole social life. However, it took a Prayerbook Mission Week to help me realise that Christianity cannot be inherited. To the surprise of most members, I admitted that I had not understood the basics of the Christian Gospel and had not given my life over to Christ.

The resulting change was remarkable. Everything I knew so well seemed new again, as if I had never really heard any of it before.

From that time on, I took seriously the need to take time to be alone with God, to read the Bible and learn to pray. I made a small table beside my bed to kneel at and the battles began. I've always found it difficult to keep up the discipline of real prayer over a long period, but in those days I used to manage it most of the time. I learned a great deal about God and he seemed very close.

Later, when I was out earning my living in London, I found a much better solution for me. An office lunch hour is an ideal period of time to be alone and there are a remarkable number of churches still open and available for prayer. I used to grab a sandwich on my way, and then spend the rest of the time quietly reading and listening to what the Lord had to say.

The only hazards were well-meaning clergy coming to ask if I was alright (full marks to them for caring enough to ask) and the odd drunk using the church for a quiet sleep.

Once or twice a week I used to use my lunch hour in this way and I still remember them as high points. I particularly recall reading large chunks of Isaiah at one go. I was bowled over by the beauty of the words, the richness of the message and the power of his vision of God.

On top of this, I used to feel the need for a special day of reckoning. A whole day, probably a Saturday, set aside for self-examination before God. I had a little book, given to me at my Confirmation. It helped concentrate my thoughts and make me aware of just how holy God is and how far short of his standards we fall. It had a section of meditations on the ten commandments and I would work my way through these, trying to be honest and look my faults straight between the eyes. The whole process helped to keep short accounts with God and the sense of forgiveness, cleanness and joy afterwards, was wonderful.

The other high point in prayer was the feeling of oneness and purpose that came from meeting to pray with other students through an organisation called Inter-Colleges Christian Fellowship (a branch of UCCF). I went on several weekends with this group when I was a student. The excitement of meeting so many young Christians from widely differing backgrounds and denominations made our times of prayer some of the best I have ever experienced.

But I don't want to give the entirely false impression that my past prayer life has been consistently rosy and fulfilling. Far from it. I more often lose the battle with laziness than win it. There have been long periods when prayer has seemed mechanical and dry. But there are always new beginnings and new initiatives too.

I know there are two opposite and conflicting forces at work when we pray. They can be felt almost physically sometimes. There is the odd reluctance we feel when the opportunity to pray present itself. A kind of resistance, together with a sudden interest in a hundred and one other things that could also be done in the time available.

Opposed to this comes the desire to pray more and to know God better, the longing to spend time with him and to know exactly what he wants in any given situation. It seems that the old battle between good and evil still rages over the times we spend in prayer. This must be some indication of how important an activity it is.

Somehow, over the years, a kind of legalism crept into my approach to times of quiet with God. The gap between the ideal 'Quiet Time', put up by well-meaning Christians and my efforts, seemed to grow so wide that my bad conscience became a burden. Typically, I rationalised the situation. We are not called to legalism. Nowhere in the Bible does it say we must spend an hour every morning in prayer. God does not work that way anyway. He treats us as individuals in a relationship of love.

Also, at about this time, I was working as a housekeeper at a church in the East End of London and realised just how culturally conditioned our ideas of Bible Study and prayer can be. There are many young Christians unaccustomed to reading and study in any form. We may be guilty of loading them with unnecessary burdens when we expect them to follow the patterns of middle-class Christianity. Reading and discussing the Bible together and praying together too, may be a much more helpful pattern to adopt, given these circumstances. Now there is much truth in all this, but it has its dangers. For someone as lacking in discipline as myself, it spells disaster. From that point on, my prayer life has been very poor, patchy and undisciplined.

Getting married, with its consequent change of living habits and greater sharing of personal things, has made some changes, but not as many as we might have hoped with all our good intentions.

We find it very hard to pray regularly together. Malcolm and I do pray about everything important to us and of course God is the head of our marriage in a very real way. However, we're not great ones for discussing every little thing together. As a result we tend to increase each other's lack of resolve, not spur each other on to greater effort.

Our involvement with our local church, however, has been a great encouragement and help in this area. The weekly Bible study group, made up of all sorts of people drawn from our immediate neighbourhood, is a joy. After talking over the passage from the Bible set for the week, we pool items for prayer from our own lives, mention anyone else that we know is in any kind of need and generally share what's going on in our world. This supportive group of friends is really helpful and as we see answers to our prayers, each one has learned a little more faith in the power of prayer and the care God has for us.

When our first baby came, we hit an all-time low. She was not an easy-going baby. She cried and yelled, demanded to be in a constant state of motion and refused to sleep. Prayer, on our part, was reduced to truly desperate pleas for help. Yet that kind of prayer, too, is an acknowledgement of utter dependence upon God, which is certainly what we felt on many occasions.

We did survive and, of course, things became much easier. Time passed and the 'new parents' gradually learnt the ropes. Our most severe test to date was to come with the arrival of Lewis two years later.

By contrast with Ellie, he was a model baby, happy and contented and very easy to look after. By ten weeks we were beginning to think we'd cracked the parenthood game, when he became ill. At first we thought it was a heavy cold and the clinic dismissed him as healthy. As the week progressed we became more worried about him and took him to the GP and on to the local hospital. No-one was sure what the matter was, so we took him home again.

The next day, having just put him down to sleep in his pram,

144

I had the feeling that I should look at Lewis again. He was blue in the face and had stopped breathing. I blew into his lungs and he began to breathe again.

At that moment a member of our church arrived in his car. Gratefully I commandeered it at once and we set off for the hospital. This time they admitted Lewis immediately and tests showed that he had meningitis.

The next few days were difficult to live through. Our tiny baby was wired up to the most impressive, yet frightening, battery of technological aids a good teaching hospital can provide. The medical staff did all they could, but they were not hopeful. On that first night they told us to go home and wait for a phone call. They did not expect Lewis to last the night.

Strangely enough, I was working on a book about prayer for children at the time. I knew all the theory, how it works and why. But in these circumstances, we had to learn the real lessons. We had to put the theory into practice.

That night we were too numb and too anxious to do more than pray arrow prayers for God's help and healing. No phone call came and the next morning the baby had improved a little.

We talked about prayer then. We had to decide what to pray for. We knew two things – that God is able to heal completely but also that it might not be his will to do so. Many Christians have received the answer 'no' when they have prayed sincerely for healing. Being so aware of the theory almost meant that we could not pray at all.

Finally, we agreed. We would pray for what we wanted most of all, putting everything about the circumstances into God's hands as our loving Father, and leave it at that. No hedging, no conditional clauses, just the truth.

And we were overwhelmed by the prayer support we received, both from the Christians close to us and also from almost total strangers. Someone whom we had barely met wrote: 'One tiny baby has so often come into my mind when I've been driving or doing the house-work, that I'm sure God has reminded me of something so important that I shouldn't be allowed to forget it.'

We also learned our dependence upon others. When something like that happens, all your strength is taken up with carrying on with life, doing what must be done and coping with worry and fear. There is not much time for real prayer. But others can pray and when they do, their support can be felt in an almost physical way.

Our Church elders were prepared to come into the hospital, lay their hands on the baby and anoint him with oil, which gave us a further sense of God's care shown through his people.

Slowly, but surely, Lewis recovered. We came through the period when the hospital thought he might not be able to see, or even hear. Then that he might be handicapped as far as walking and coordination was concerned. But none of these gloomy predictions turned out to be true. Lewis came through the disease completely unscathed as far as we can tell.

Now, four years later, the kids are relatively civilised and life has returned to somewhere near what we called normality before they arrived. I feel as if I am 'me' again. I can do some work of my own, have a few more interests outside home and generally begin living again.

And now I have no excuse for my lax prayer life. What am I to do, having come through the experiences I have described and hopefully having learnt a few things on the way?

I think I must begin again, to build some discipline into my new life. I don't want to return to the old legalism, but I have learned that I don't work very well without some firm structure to keep me at it. There is a tremendous amount of truth in this observation from Thomas-à-Kempis:

> *'If you keep up the habit of retiring for prayer*
> *you will find it sweet;*
> *but if it is irregularly done*
> *a distaste for it will be the result.'*

I know God is real, that he knows all about me and my daily circumstances. And prayer is meant to be my response to him. I don't have to clock up the hours in order to please him, I don't have to twist his arm to get him involved.

He is involved already. Prayer will bring me into things with him. It will help me to know what is really going on and to be a part of it. I am free to work this out in whatever way is right for me. And I must let others do the same in their own lives.

Everyone says that we get more balanced as we get older. We are more likely to become 'middle of the road', be the peace-makers, temper our enthusiasm . . . That may be true, but there really is a lot to be said for balance at any age – as long as balance does not mean uncaring complacency. The balance between form (by which I mean structure, or discipline or underlying principle) and freedom seems to be a crucial one.

So that's my new goal. A disciplined prayer life that will leave me free to learn the next lessons in prayer that God has to teach me.

17 Eileen Vincent:
Prayer Mountain – Climbing

I was always a pray-er – although I probably wouldn't have' called it that. As a small child, I had a secret relationship with God – never talked about, but woven into the whole fabric of life. Curled up in a little ball with my head under the bed-covers I would 'say my prayers'. '*Dear Lord Jesus* . . .' and out would spill a run-through of the day's happenings. The good and the bad, the hurts and the troubles – in sadness and loneliness God was my confidant.

Certain important requests were never asked in such a casual fashion, they required a more dignified approach. Like the occasion when my sister found fleas in her hair! They had probably come from the prisoners of war whom we had been helping bring in the harvest. Straightening myself up as if walking into the throne-room of a king, and deliberately focusing all my attention on the great God in heaven, solemnly I made my request, '*Please don't let them ever come into my hair.*' To make sure the point was understood I repeated it, then told God I was leaving the prayer with him and expecting an answer.

In a childlike way I received, by faith, the assurance God had heard and years later, when in India, sitting among people crawling with head-lice, I had confidence God would still protect me! At seven years old a seed of lasting faith was planted alongside confidence in prayer. For me prayer began in childhood days as a friendship which over the years deepened with understanding, especially after I became a committed Christian. But before I say much more, let me describe what I mean by prayer.

Above everything else, it is a relationship and begins with just believing *God is* – whether I feel him near or not. Once I experienced a severe trial of faith, when outwardly it appeared God didn't answer prayer and his word was untrue, yet deep down I trusted him – it seemed impossible not to because I knew him. When I talk to him, it's to someone who is real. I feel at ease with him. I know he knows everything about me, yet loves me completely. Words are inadequate to describe the nature of this relationship. It's vital. We share life. Because prayer is based upon such intimacy, fancy words and ceremonial ways of approach seem completely inappropriate. When I pray I am talking to my father. How wrong it would be to start behaving like a stranger, using formalities or someone else's poetic turns of phrase. He would know I wasn't being real.

I talk to God about everything. Despite this, if anyone starts speaking about prayer I nearly always get a guilty feeling. Satan loves to come in and start accusing me. His attack usually emphasises that I'm not praying in the same way as someone else or another group, and certainly not praying enough. Then I start to question if my type of praying is real praying or if perhaps other people know something I don't. Satan is an expert at getting us on that treadmill.

At a large gathering in the New Forest, Arthur Wallis spoke powerfully on prayer and called the congregation to commit themselves to this privileged work for God. I remained seated. How could I stand up and make further promises to God when I already found the ones I had made too difficult to keep? Don't we all feel like that?

I have read all the best books on prayer and come to the conclusion that *one only learns to pray by praying*. I'm filled with admiration for the 'Praying Hydes' and 'Andrew Murrays', men who had notable prayer lives, but I could never quite see myself fitting into their kind of mould. At one point in my Christian life it quite troubled me as instinctively I knew a disciplined prayer life was vital. As I talked it out with the Lord I realised I would continue in dissatisfaction whilst I tried to model myself on others and become condemned in the process.

'Pray and do not faint'

At heart I'm a doer, which is about as far removed from a spiritual mystic as you can get! But prayer isn't only for spiritual mystics, it's for everyone and all types. I can't imagine myself not being busy, with a home, a husband, children and a thousand and one demands in an active church life. Probably your days are much the same. Given opportunity, the devil attempts to use this bustle to his advantage, suggesting that my hectic life-style is a legitimate reason for not praying. If that's the truth, then most women haven't time for prayer. But the devil's a liar and always has been.

So I must not allow prayer to be constantly postponed to some convenient time like 'when the baby goes to nursery school', or when 'the children grow up'. The convenient time will never come. We are eternal optimists always expecting the future will produce more time. I have learned not to wait – but to get on and pray. The future is not going to produce more time.

'When you pray'

I can hear you asking, 'Well, how am I to pray?' It's simple – start talking to God. He's there on tiptoes waiting to hear you! Now I know it says in the Bible, '*Go into your room and shut the door and pray*'; well, not everyone has got a room or a door to shut. It's not always simple to get away.

Solitude is an ideal but not essential and sometimes unobtainable. Hubbub and hurly-burly need not mean no prayer. We must train our minds to constantly be in tune with God.

Communion is the word which sums up this relationship. You can have the most perfect conditions of quiet and seclusion but fail to have communion – a real meeting with God, where you give and receive. When my spirit is aware and open I talk, so to speak, face to face with God and come away with a fresh infusion of life. Then I know all the wonderful things the Bible says about me are true: I'm an overcomer, accepted in the Beloved, precious and loved. Power flows into every area of my life. But how this quality of prayer is contested by the devil; he would do anything to keep us from it. At times it seems God gets lost in a fog, we could call it the devil's smoke-screen; I've learned that it's essential then to persist until communion is achieved. How do I do it? First recognise the enemy – tell him to go and deliberately praise the Lord till the fog clears.

The busy young mum may find real communion in prayer whilst she feeds the baby, but if it's her second and she is harassed by a jealous toddler she will have to train her mind to commune and pray whilst involved with more active occupations. It's amazing how practised we can become at praying on the run whilst pushing the hoover or hanging out the nappies!

I want to encourage all who find life far from ideal not to count

151

themselves out but rather to find a way *through* to a meaningful prayer life tailor-made to circumstances.

Over the years I have trained my mind so that I can be alone with God, although with others. By perseverance it's possible to cultivate this way of living. The verse 'Pray without ceasing', always challenged me. I knew I couldn't be on my knees all the time, but God meant what he said. Then understanding dawned; with the injunction, he has also shown us how. The key lies in a life of communion.

I wouldn't want you to get the impression that there is a switch that can be thrown which makes everything automatic. No, discipline is required. When I open my eyes in the morning my first thoughts are of the Lord. If it isn't automatic I make it deliberate. I *turn* my heart to God.

I never like to talk when I first wake. Talking seems to set the day in motion. Once the radio goes on and conversations begin, it is almost impossible to recapture the special blessing of the new day. My first words are always reserved for the Lord and as the day proceeds there are many occasions when I again consciously turn from earthly entanglements to pray.

Pray in the Spirit

It's impossible to talk about prayer without discussing the gift of tongues. I cannot set too high a value upon this beautiful gift. What a privilege to speak to God in the Spirit! – even though I cannot understand with my mind. Many times as I turn to the Lord in prayer the way into his conscious presence is by first praying in tongues. The gift seems to open the door of my inner spirit, setting me free to behave like a spiritual being, so that I can commune with the Spirit of the almighty God. It's an alarm bell to my spiritual system, waking me up and causing me to be alert to the presence of God. It opens my ears so that I am sensitised to the loving whispers of my heavenly Father. Surely so often tongues is the language of love between two spiritual beings. How easily worship flows, and with it, the awareness that God hears.

We all want to know that God hears our prayers. When doubt seeps in, and it seems that the wall-paper has soaked up every word, the whole activity appears futile. Then worship takes on a new importance and acts as a dam to keep out doubt. John 9.31

152

says, 'If anyone is a worshipper of God and does his will, God listens to him'.

There are times when I do not know how to pray. I am genuinely not in possession of all the facts or feel my own motives could be suspect – I want God's will but am not sure what it is. At such times I yield my whole will to God and pray in tongues. It may seem incomprehensible that praying in a language that I do not understand brings clarity to my thoughts – but it does. As the Spirit prays through me, he sorts out attitudes and motives and brings revelation into muddled situations. Instead of my trying to work it out, God clears the confusion and shows me how to pray with understanding.

Hearing God

Prayer does not achieve God's full purpose in our lives if it only remains at the level of relationship and communion. The delightful security of knowing God, sharing everything with him and seeing his provision is only an initial stage in a prayer life. Prayer can develop into a work for God.

God's purpose is done in our own lives and on earth as we pray – asking him to do his will. To the natural mind that is a very strange concept; but *God has limited himself to our asking.* So to ask for the right things it is essential to develop the dimension of hearing God in our prayers. Prayer is a two-way business. Time must be given to listening and hearing. I find life dry and hard when I fail in this area. God is always waiting to speak but sadly I don't always stop to listen.

I can almost hear someone asking, 'But how do you know it's God?' You don't at first. It all works by faith. You believe that the thought or words that suddenly came into your mind are God speaking. They come as an impression, or a word, or a prompting to read certain scriptures, even an an audible voice, although that has never happened to me. But you can be sure, whatever God says is never at variance with his word. This is our safeguard. Every nudge of the Spirit can be checked out against the nature of God, the plan and ordained order given to us in the Bible.

It is only as we act upon the words God speaks to us, in whatever form they come, that they are revealed to be the truth. I had an amusing experience many years ago when I had seen a beautiful table for sale second-hand. It was a bargain, but I hesitated to buy. I asked the Lord about it as I was fearful it would be too large. Then, reading the Bible whilst lying in the bath the words, '*Buy up every opportunity*' seemed to stand out from the page. I knew (by faith) God was saying, '*Buy the table*'. Without any further hesitation we hurried to the house and triumphantly returned with the table which matched our other furniture and fitted perfectly!

The word of God is an indispensible aid to our prayer life. It's there, in the pages of the Bible that we learn of God's will. As we read, we more clearly understand the way we should pray. Prayer and Bible reading go arm in arm for me. What I read triggers off my thoughts for prayer and what I pray gives me deeper understanding of the word.

In the natural, we stop and listen when important topics are being discussed; so how much more should we be prepared to cultivate a listening spirit when God wants to share momentous issues with his people? At such times 'prayer on the run' is like chatter and quite inadequate. We live in the last days when to know how and what to pray is essential. Only then we can pray aright and co-operate with God's purpose for our generation.

It's one thing to have our heavenly Father meet our daily needs but quite another to become his co-worker through whom he can pray and meet the needs of a whole sin-sick world. God is looking for prayer partners.

Prayer Mountain

In 1982 I visited Full Gospel Central Church in Korea – the largest church in the world, with the fantastic congregation of three hundred and fifty thousand people. It is not surprising to find fervent commitment to prayer at the very heart of the church. My most memorable experience was at Prayer Mountain, a retreat centre where throughout the year thousands gather to pray day and night. The place was charged with a strange atmosphere so that I felt as if I had entered another world and was a spectator to many things I didn't understand. From behind the closed doors of small prayer rooms flowed a continuous torrent of prayer. I felt humbled in the presence of those who were able to pray for hours and hours alone and who thought little of remaining in the prayer rooms all night. Desperately I tried to pray as burdens weighed heavily upon my own heart, but found I was ill-practised

154

at 'getting-through' – at sustaining prayer till I felt free from the heaviness of heart.

These Korean Christians have given themselves to a spirit of prayer. Ceaselessly they call upon God to bring his rule into their land. I found it incredibly difficult to persevere with my own prayer burdens for even one hour, but they have broken through the spiritual opposition and intend to overthrow Satan, who controls men's lives and keeps them captive in the kingdom of darkness.

Two-thirds of those gathered at Prayer Mountain were women, many with babies tied on their backs. They had left their home responsibilities to come to an inhospitable place in freezing temperatures for prayer and fasting. Fasting expressed their attitude to God, '*Lord, whatever it costs us, let your will be done on earth*'. The gates of hell cannot resist this continual bombardment. Korea enjoys a continuing outpouring of the Holy Spirit, daily hundreds are being saved, healed and delivered.

When you fast

Fasting is not a way of twisting God's arm; it's a declaration that I'm prepared to back my words with an attitude of death to self. I still don't find it easy to fast but at least I'm not sick, as at my first attempt! Then I decided to miss breakfast and lunch and eat again at 3.30 in the afternoon. For the whole day I seemed to do nothing but think about food – prayer was impossible. In the afternoon visitors came and my mind was occupied dreaming of making them a cup of tea and cake at 3.30. On the dot I produced the refreshments, gulped mine down and was promptly sick! I'm happy to say I've progressed a little since then, but the determination required to decide to fast never seems to become easier. By the time we get to fasting about a situation a shift in emphasis in our praying has usually taken place. No longer is it our prayer we want answered, but God's will done. Slowly the two become synonymous.

Fasting is not a legal extravagance of the zealous pray-er. Jesus said, '*WHEN you fast*', not 'if you fast'. It's a fruitful obedience in the life of the Christian, causing the spirit to be more finely tuned. Fasting speaks powerfully into the spiritual realm, it's an identification with the cross which declares to the powers of darkness that they must yield to the rule of Christ.

At a prayer meeting in my home church we had a prophecy saying God had given us a two-edged sickle with which to reap – one blade was prayer, the other fasting. Used together, certainly we will bring in the harvest.

Notice it is prayer with fasting. We need to keep this powerful combination together and make time whilst we fast and work, to also pray.

I really want to impress upon you that the ministry of prayer is not only for 'Super Saints' – if it was, you could count me out, and the thousands of ordinary women in Korea who spend their time fasting and praying as well. They too have problems and difficulties. Their days have to stretch across mundane chores without the aid of modern gadgets and machines. Many of them are fairly new converts and certainly do not have the wealth of books and teaching that are available in Western countries. We know so much – but they are doing it.

Faith in prayer

Whilst in Korea, although I felt inadequate in prayer, something happened in my heart giving me a new vital knowledge that God works through prayer. Someone once said, 'Why worry when you can pray?' I realised so much of my time spent thinking was really worrying; now in a deliberate way – I pray, and know God will work.

Like most of us, I have lists of recurring prayer needs. One is tempted to wonder why God doesn't answer but his silences do not cause me to doubt, I know his faithfulness, God will work in response to prayer. With new persistence I keep on praying.

As never before I feel an urgency to pray. Time is short, Jesus is going to return and we, his people, must watch and pray. He wants to teach us proficiency in prayer warfare and expand our faith. Then he can use us to establish the Kingdom of God. Personally I find praying with others releases me into a greater liberty in prayer. Then it is so much easier to believe and overcome.

Our church encourages prayer in small groups. Friends together learn to pray by praying. Collectively we experience release in prayer rarely known when alone, this develops each of us individually. We have found meeting regularly essential to forge bonds in prayer. I meet with two other housewives, and what love and power flows from our weekly hour together! We've seen answers to prayer and learned how to bear one another's burdens. Alone I can chase a thousand but together we chase ten thousand.

In 1968, with my husband, I attended the fourth Chakestan Baptist Convention, a tribal affair in the far North-East corner of India. With two and a half thousand others I sat on the ground when the leader said, 'Shall we pray'. From all around me a growing thunderous roar went up as everyone opened their mouths and prayed. I was staggered at the noise and abandonment in prayer. After a few minutes it subsided and the meeting continued. It had been an awesome experience to be *drowned* in prayer! I sat wondering. It seemed to me that these primitive people had done more praying in those five minutes than some churches in a year.

Prayer meetings in Korea follow the same pattern. One topic after another is announced and prayed by the leader. Then the whole congregation, twelve thousand people at the all-night prayer meeting, lift their voices together and call upon God, just as the early church did in Acts 4. Once a month our whole church comes together to pray. In these gatherings we pray like the Chakestan and Koreans. It means everyone can pray rather than wait and listen to others. It keeps the meeting alive and moving, but most of all its worth is proved by many immediate answers to prayer.

All praying is a mysterious activity of faith. We speak out the truths God has declared in his word and by faith believe that he will act on our behalf. Our prayers are asking him to do what he has said he would do. Strangely, declaring by faith God's truth is our means to overthrow Satan. It's an unusual way to fight a war, but powerfully effective.

Praying is something that all believers can do. No one will see; it is done in secret and its victories are often veiled from our eyes. No bouquets are given to pray-ers, but I wouldn't be surprised if front seats have not been reserved for them in heaven.

In Queen Esther's day the call to prayer went out because a nation was in peril. Today, our danger is as great and the Spirit is sounding out the alert; Come women of God, let's pray!